150 YEARS OF CRIME & PUNISHMENT IN WESTERN NEW YORK

Revised 2nd Edition

MICHAEL T. KEENE

WM

Revised Second Edition Published by Willow Manor Publishing

Fredericksburg, VA 22406

www.WillowManorPublishing.com

Illustrations courtesy of MS Illustrations and Ad-Hoc Productions

Cover images courtesy of Ad-Hoc Productions & the Rochester

Museum & Science Center

First published 2012 by CJM Books

Revised Second Edition published 2013 by Willow Manor Publishing

Manufactured in the United States

LCCN 2013948564

Library of Congress Catalogue-in-Publication Data

Keene, Michael.

Murder, Mayhem and Madness: 150 Years of Crime & Punishment
in Western, New York

Michael Keene

p.cm.

Includes bibliographic references.

ISBN 978-1-939688-06-4

1.Murders—New York (state)—Western New York. 2. History—New York (state)—
Western New York. 3. Stories—New York (state)—Western New York. 4. Crime—New York
(state)—Western New York. 5. Capital Punishment—New York (state)—Western New York.

Anecdotes. I. Title

Contents

Introduction

In the process of writing my first book, *The Mystery of Hoodoo Corner & Other Tales,* I came across many interesting stories of murder and mayhem in New York State. Some of them were included — or at least mentioned — in that first book, though not in the kind of detail I wanted, and others didn't touch on my main story. But I gathered the material as I went along and long before I finished that book, I began thinking about a second.

This collection of thirteen stories runs from the eighteenth century to the early twentieth century, about 150 years in all. All are murders that took place in, or are otherwise connected to, Western New York. In many small towns, it sometimes seems as if "nothing" ever happens, that life is slow and calm, and, usually, it is. But in even the smallest hamlet — or perhaps in a train station — shocking crimes occur. The stories sometimes live on as legend, sometimes not.

As I did before, I included primary source material whenever possible. I have used mostly newspaper accounts, but also personal letters and court transcripts. Hearing the words of the victims, the perpetrators, and of those who dealt with them, such as judges and police officers, lends a depth and integrity to these stories that cannot be gained by any other method.

Through a sampling of murder and mayhem during a century and a half, it is easy to see the truth of the adage: Times change, people don't.

Chapter 1
The Torture Tree

Today a small town of about 2,500 residents, the western New York town of Leicester was, until the American Revolution, a major stronghold of the Seneca. Three major Seneca villages were located in the area: Little Beard's Town, Big Tree, and Squakie Hill. Now, just off US–20A, there are two parks —one state, one town— both bearing the names of Boyd–Parker. A little blue sign at the entrance to the state park, consisting of fifteen words —"Torture Tree and Burial Mound/Western Limit Sullivan's Expedition 1779/Seneca Village Little Beardstown"— does an admirable, if limited, job of  conveying the highlights of one of the most gruesome stories to come out of the Revolutionary War era. The story of what happened to Lieutenant Thomas Boyd and Sergeant Michael Parker was followed by grave robbery, accusations of conspiracy, and the burial and reburial of human remains for nearly twenty-five years.

First, some background. In 1777 the Continental Congress, concerned that a major Indian war was imminent, decided to raise an army of three thousand men to deal with the Indian problem on the frontier. (At the time, the frontier ran roughly along the modern Ohio–Pennsylvania border and was bounded on the south by the Ohio River.) Planning and preparations were slow, and the campaign would take nearly a year to be brought to fruition. But the course of events during that year only hardened the resolve of the Americans. Indian–Loyalist attacks on settlers continued apace. There were some reprisals by American units already in the field, but the small number of available troops made it nearly impossible to offer an effective defense, or to thwart the ability of the Indians and Loyalists to mount attacks.

This became clear in November 1778, when nearly four hundred Seneca Indians, led by Cornplanter, launched on assault on a fort near Cherry Valley. The so-called Cherry Valley Massacre—in which approximately fifty soldiers and civilians died, with another eighty taken captive—forced the hand of the fledgling American government.

Thus, General George Washington assigned Major General John Sullivan to lead the force to deal with the Seneca. The Sullivan Expedition, as this campaign would come to be known, was notorious for the toll it took on both sides. In the end, Col. Sullivan had nearly four thousand men at his command, and he drove them—and their horses—tirelessly. The village of Horseheads, located in the Southern Tier of New York, acquired its name from an event during this campaign. The packhorses of Sullivan's army, having hauled heavy military equipment for over four hundred miles through difficult terrain, reached the end of their endurance in a little valley, and there the horses were slaughtered en masse. A few years later, horse skulls were arrayed along the trail by returning Native Americans, reportedly as a warning, or as a gesture of anger or defiance.

By early September 1779, General John Sullivan and his men had already had two significant engagements. On September 11th, his army was camped about a mile from the head of the Conesus Lake and the men constructed a bridge to take artillery over the water. The immediate objective was Genesee Castle, the principal Seneca village in the area. Sullivan's map said that it was on the east bank of the river, while Indian guides said that it was on the west

The Sullivan Expedition Monument in Mount Hope Cemetery marks the final resting place of Lt. Boyd, Sgt. Parker and their companions.

bank. To settle the matter, Gen. Sullivan instructed Lieutenant Thomas Boyd, of Morgan's Riflemen, to put together a small scouting party and find the Indian village. He was instructed to locate the village and report back with the best route to it. Boyd did not follow Sullivan's order, however, and assembled a party of approximately twenty-seven men (the numbers vary slightly in accounts), and an Indian guide, Oneida chief Hanyost Thaosagwat. The party departed at approximately 11:00 P.M.

From almost the very start, things went wrong. As Gen. Sullivan would later write in a report to his superiors:

> *Lieutenant Boid* [sic] *was the officer entrusted with this service, who took with him twenty-three men, volunteers from the same corps, and a few from Colonel Butler's regiment, making in all*

twenty-six, a much larger number than I had thought of sending... The guides were by no means acquainted with the country, mistook the road in the night, and at daybreak fell in with a castle six miles higher up than Chenesee, inhabited by a tribe called Squatchegas. Here they saw a few Indians, killed and scalped two, the rest fled. Two runners were immediately dispatched to me with the account and informed that the party was on their return.

When the bridge was almost completed some of them came in and told us that Lieutenant [Boyd] and men of his party were almost surrounded by the enemy; that the enemy had been discovering themselves before him for some miles; that his men had killed two and were eagerly pursuing the rest; but soon found themselves almost surrounded by three or four hundred Indians and rangers. Those of Mr. Boid's men who were sent to secure his flanks fortunately made their escape; but he with fourteen of his party and the Oneida chief being in the centre, were completely encircled. The light troops of the army and the flanking divisions were immediately detached to their relief; but arrived too late, the enemy having destroyed the party and escaped.

Although Boyd and Parker had not found the village that was their target, —they, in fact, found the village of Gathtsegwarohare, which had been abandoned— Boyd initially decided, after sending back a small party, to wait for the army to join him. After they left, four Indians on horseback rode into the village. Boyd attacked, killing one Indian and wounding another. The wounded Indian and two others escaped. Boyd decided to turn his men back toward the main body of Sullivan's army and after a few miles, Boyd sent two men ahead, to reach them more quickly. The men soon returned, after sighting five Indians on the path, who swiftly fled. Reportedly, the Indian guide told Boyd that it was a trap — a set-up for an ambush — but he ignored the advice. Boyd and his men led pursuit, not realizing that they were about to come in contact with about four hundred Indians and Tories. The men had been lying in wait, to ambush Sullivan's Army as it approached, up a steep hill from Conesus Lake. Thus, Boyd's party was led directly into the enemy's lines and surrounded. In hearing Boyd's men firing, some Indians believed the ambush had begun and fired upon another surveying party that was coming up from Conesus Lake. Boyd's men fought for some time and finally made their way to a small grove of trees. Though the precise numbers vary, the best estimate is that eighteen were killed there, while two were captured and five escaped.

Upon hearing the gunfire, Sullivan dispatched the Light Corps and flanking divisions of General Hand's Third Brigade to reinforce Boyd's men, but they arrived too late. The Indians were already in retreat to the west. General Sullivan immediately dispatched reinforcements. The reinforcements encountered a few Indian warriors who offered resistance and were quickly killed, but the main portion of the Indian party was gone. They had fled along the river to Genesee Castle. The Indians believed, when they'd encountered Boyd and Parker's party, that they'd in fact encountered Sullivan's Army itself, for which they had prepared a huge ambush, concealing themselves in ravines, waiting to attack the army as it passed by. But the larger party of Indians, hearing fierce fighting at their rear, believed that they were surrounded and abandoned their positions. When they realized later that the fight was with a small scouting party, the element of surprise they'd depended on for their large-scale ambush was gone, besides the fact that it was nearly impossible to reassemble and reinsert the large number of warriors. This, in addition to what Boyd and Parker endured, accounts for the oft-told nature of this story. Boyd and his men might in fact have saved Sullivan's Army from decimation at Seneca hands.

To return to the story, Sullivan describes what was found when reinforcements arrived:

> *It appears that our men had taken to a small grove, the ground around it being clear on every side for several rods, and there fought till Mr. Boid was shot through the body, and his men all killed except one, who, with his wounded commander was made prisoner. The firing was so close, before this brave party were destroyed, that the powder of the enemy's muskets was driven into their flesh. In this conflict the enemy must have suffered greatly, as they had no cover, and our men were possessed of a very advantageous one. This advantage of ground and the obstinate bravery of the party, with some other*

circumstances, induced me to believe their loss must have been very considerable. They were so long employed in removing and secreting their dead, that the advance of General Hand's party obliged them to leave one alongside the riflemen, and at least a wagon load of packs, blankets, hats and provisions, which they had thrown off to enable them to act with more agility in the field.

On September 14, Sullivan and his army arrived at a deserted Genesee Castle, where they found the bodies of Boyd and Parker. It was apparent that they had been tortured. Sullivan wrote:

Another reason which induces me to suppose they suffered much was the unparalleled tortures they inflicted upon the brave and unfortunate Boid, [whose] body, with that of the equally unfortunate companion, we found at Chinesee. [Genesee Castle.] It appeared that they had whipped them in the most cruel manner, pulled out Mr. Boid's nails, cut off his nose, plucked out one of his eyes, cut out his tongue, stabbed him with spears in sundry places, and inflicted other tortures which decency will not permit me to mention; lastly, cut off his head, and left his body on the ground with that of his unfortunate companion, who appeared to have experienced nearly the same savage barbarity....

The "unparalleled tortures" that "decency" would not permit Sullivan to mention were nevertheless recorded in the diaries of other men in the party. Lieutenant Erkuries Beatty, of the Fourth Pennsylvania Regiment, wrote:

Tuesday 14th. [O]n entering the town we found the body of Lt. Boyd and another Rifle Man in a most terrible mangled condition. They were both stripped naked and their heads Cut off and the flesh of Lt. Boyd's head was [e]ntirely taken of and his eyes punched out. The other man's head was not there. They was stab[b]ed I sup[p]ose in 40 different places in the Body with a spear and great gashes cut in their flesh with

The Torture Tree

Two men are seated on the base of the Boyd Monument at the head of Conesus Lake. Boyd was horribly tortured and killed at "The Torture Tree" along with Sgt. Michael Parker.

> *knifes, and Lt. Boyd's Privates was nearly cut of & hanging down, his finger and Toe nails was bruised of and the Dogs had eat part of their Shoulders away likewise a knife was Sticking in Lt. Boyd's body. They was i[m]mediately buried with the honour of war.* [sic]

Upon their capture, Boyd, Parker, and their Indian guide had been taken to Little Beard's Town (now Cuylerville.) They were questioned by Joseph Brant, a Mohawk Indian with an English name and a fierce reputation gained in his savage attacks on American settlements, John Butler, an American loyal to the Crown who led the Tory Rangers, and Chief Little Beard of the Seneca. According to some accounts, Boyd and Parker did not talk, bearing torture without revealing anything of value to the enemy. But a report that Butler sent to the British Army shortly thereafter gave accurate information about Sullivan's troops, their movements, and supplies and armaments. So it may not be true that Boyd and/or Parker withstood the torture inflicted on them. In fact, in his correspondence, Butler refers to Boyd as "very intelligent," suggesting that he was present as Boyd was interrogated. Butler, however, makes no mention of Boyd's fate. Reportedly, when Bryant and Butler were done with their interrogation, they left, leaving the fate of the two American soldiers in the hands of Chief Little Beard and his men.

Boyd and Parker were taken to a large oak tree and stripped naked. They were then whipped until their backs were covered with welts and bruises. Next the nails were pulled from each finger and toe. Their right ears were cut off, then their noses, then their tongues. Their right eyes were gouged from their sockets, and left hanging. Their genitals were mutilated, eventually held to their bodies only by a strand of flesh. Such torture is designed to keep the victims alive and conscious as long as possible, so that they might suffer. The final acts of cruelty came when the two men had their abdomens cut open and their intestines removed. The severed end was fastened to the tree and the men were driven around the tree, their intestines being pulled out as they went.

Their hearts were ripped from their chests. Finally, they were beheaded. Reportedly, Boyd's head was placed on a spear and used to lead a dance around the tree. Later, his partially-skinned head was found on a log. Parker's head was never found.

Sullivan's men buried the bodies at the junction of two small creeks, about fifty feet from the tree. Boyd and Parker remained interred by the Torture Tree, apparently undisturbed for over thirty years. Then, in 1807, robbers looted the graves, taking clothing as relics. In 1830, the grave was opened again and four Revolutionary Army uniform buttons were found, authenticating the site. In 1841, the bones were disinterred and the bones of Boyd and Parker were placed in a wooden urn[1] and those of the others, including some of Boyd's men

The Torture Tree marks the farthest point west General Sullivan's army marched. In 1927 the Livingston County Historical Society dedicated the tree as part of the Boyd and Parker Memorial Park.

buried at Groveland, were put in a wooden box. In August of that year, six canal boats filled with five military companies, invited guests, and journalists went down the Genesee Valley Canal to Cuylerville to bring the remains back to Rochester's new Mount Hope Cemetery. The ceremony there was hosted by New York Governor William H. Seward. The two receptacles containing the bones were placed on Patriot Hill, also known as Revolutionary Hill.

It is said that emotions ran so high that descendants of the 1807 grave robbers even returned some of the artifacts that had been stolen. In any case, in Rochester, with due ceremony, the wooden urn and sarcophagus were placed next to a temporary wooden monument in Mount Hope Cemetery. The very next day the Democrats accused the Whigs of burying the bones of a bear rather than the remains of Boyd and Parker. The controversy raged for years, in spite of the fact that those at the Cuylerville watched as the original grave was opened.

Meanwhile, the wooden urn and sarcophagus sat on the ground, exposed to Rochester's weather, and the urn was overturned during a violent storm. A cemetery caretaker saw the bones lying on the ground and buried them. Then, during the Civil War, when the city was strapped for cash and in need of burial plots for the poor, it leveled Patriot Hill, sold some of the lots, and removed the remains to a nearby potter's field, a public burial spot for the indigent.[2] Finally, in 1903, members of the Irondequoit chapter of the Daughters of the American Revolution found the remains in potter's field and they were reburied, again. Today, that burial site is marked with a granite boulder and a bronze plaque.

Thus, today, there are scattered sites to visit. There is a small park with a monument at the site the ambush outside of Groveland, New York. The monument lists the names of the soldiers killed,[3] and a plate bearing the name of the Oneida Indian guide, Han Yost has recently been added. The Torture Tree itself is a large bur oak located in a small park near the site of the Seneca Castle, of Little Beards Town. It also marks the farthest point west that General Sullivan's army marched. On September 15, 1779, after these events, the army began their return.

Chapter 2
The Man Who Was Hanged Twice

Today, Caledonia is a small town with 4,500 residents. Its claim to fame is that it was once the home of Cornplanter, the Seneca leader. It began the nineteenth century as a small settlement called Southhampton. The name gives a clue to its settler origins: "Caledonia" is the Latin word for Scotland, a fitting name for a town built up by Scottish settlers, growing outward from two springs that flowed into a small pond. In 1805, John Cameron moved to the community from Geneva and opened a tavern called "Springs." It's there that our story begins. On the afternoon of March 16, 1807, James McLean and William Orr were drinking together in the tavern.

The men left—drinking during the working day was then quite common—to go back to work, building a nearby road with another neighbor, Archibald McLaughlin. As Lockwood Lyon Doty, a local historian, wrote, the events of that afternoon "filled the infant settlement with horror, and made a deep impression on many."[4] McLean and Orr soon fell into a dispute. It just so happened that the road they were working on ran by the McColl home. Donald

The Man Who Was Hanged Twice

McColl, a boy of sixteen, happened to be clearing brush at the time, saw the events clearly, and would later testify to them. Doty described it this way:

> *McLean grew enraged and suddenly raised his axe and cleft Orr's skull, killing him almost instantly. Archibald McLaughlin came up a moment after, and stooping down to look at the murdered man, exclaimed in a tone of reproach, 'Oh...what have you done now!' Without any further provocation he [McLean] raised his axe again, and striking McLaughlin on the shoulder, cut him down to the very heart. Donald McColl...with great boldness and dexterity jerked the axe off McLean's shoulder and hid it in a thick jungle of hazel bushes. He then fled, as for his life, to the village. McLean pursued him until he found he could not overtake him, and then he hid himself. Meanwhile Donald McColl reached the village frightened almost out of his senses, and gave the alarm. The whole settlement was roused to arrest the murdered.*

McLean initially managed to elude his pursuers, a militia led by Judge Ezra Platt, by hiding in the forest. He allegedly secretly received food from his mother. About three weeks later, McLean was captured, but not by the small squads that were still searching for him. He was at a tavern in Canandaigua and was recognized by the landlady, who noted McLean's unusually long arms (his hands were said to fall below his knees), which had been noted in the "Wanted" poster. She also noticed McLean's keen interest in reading the "Wanted" poster hanging on the wall of her establishment. She notified Sheriff Benjamin Barton, who arrested McLean and jailed him in Batavia.

The Trial

In June 1807, McLean was put on trial for the murder of William Orr. McLean was not charged in the murder of McLaughlin, apparently because the prosecution believed that the defense might have argued successfully that Orr was responsible for McLaughlin's death. Or perhaps the prosecution felt that one successful conviction would suit their purposes, as they were seeking the

17

death penalty. The facts of the case were not much in dispute, then or now. Today, the case is well-remembered for another reason: James McLean was not only the first man to be hanged in Genesee County, but he was hanged twice. In fact, the only real point of contention is: What exactly did James McLean say when the rope broke?

At trial, both Mrs. McColl and her son, Duncan, eyewitnesses, testified to the events leading to the murders of the two men. Mrs. McColl was standing in front of the cabin while her son cleared brush nearby. She believed the

In 1807, Caledonia, New York, was the scene of a double murder where James McLean axed two of his neighbors to death over a land dispute.

argument broke out over William Orr's felling of a whitewood tree on land which had been claimed by McLean. Other witnesses said that all three men were in fact squatters on land known as the "Forty Thousand Acre Tract," and that all three had been clearing land to build the new road.

It was well-known that the Scottish community in the area was generally divided into two groups: the Inverness group, which was comprised of the newly-arrived and relatively wealthier group who had purchased property outright, and the Pertshire group, which was comprised of those who had arrived and settled some time earlier on lands known as the "Donation Lands." Thus the Pertshire group was, in effect, squatters, who nevertheless worked hard to improve the land they claimed as their own. But the extra-legality of these claims led to considerable strife and disagreement between these two groups, giving rise to numerous arguments.[5] The evidence suggests that James McLean and Archibald McLaughlin (the second victim) were both of the Pertshire group, while William Orr, the first victim, was from the Inverness group.

In any case, Mrs. McColl said McLean raised his broad axe and struck William Orr four times, including two fatal blows to the throat, one in the left shoulder, and one in the left side. When McLaughlin reproached McLean, he too was struck down. One fatal blow to the upper back was reported as "cutting him down to the very heart."[6] Such a rendering may be rhetorical flourish, as the coroner's report lists four wounds, none more than two inches deep. It notes as well that Orr sustained two "fatal" wounds, with "a certain axe made of Iron and Steel of the value of fifty cents."[7]

Both victims apparently died instantly.

James McLean was found guilty of the murder of Orr and ordered to hang by the neck until dead.

The Execution

James McLean was hung August 28th, 1807 by Sheriff Benjamin Barton in front of a great crowd that gathered to see the first public execution in Genesee County, New York.

On that day, McLean was hung using a new type of apparatus, rather than what came to be known as the conventional gallows, when man was dropped through a trapdoor. In this method, the condemned stood on the ground and a rope—tied to a weight, which was held in place by a bracket—was affixed around his neck. When the weight was dropped, the condemned was hoisted into the air. It was intended to break the neck, as all hanging gallows are intended to do, but if it didn't, the man would strangle to death. [8]

On this day, when the weight was dropped, McLean was hoisted into the air. But the rope broke, dropping him down onto the ground again — stunned, but very much alive.

Thus was born a story that has been told and retold, such that the truth of what was said by whom has been lost in the mists of time. In one version, McLean eventually got to his feet and said he didn't want to be hanged again. Nevertheless, a county clerk was dispatched to fetch another rope. During the wait, in another version, McLean remarked, "As I killed two men, I deserve two hangings." In yet another version, McLean protested a second hanging since he'd been sentenced to be hanged, and he had been. It wasn't his fault, he argued, if it didn't take.

It is clear that a debate broke out amongst the spectators. Some said McLean had been convicted of one murder and had already been hung for that, insisting that one hanging was a fulfillment of the law. Others, however, thought differently and informed McLean that "as he had killed two men, he ought to be hung twice." McLean had in fact been tried and convicted of killing one man.

In any case, the county clerk soon returned with a rope sufficiently strong and after considerable delay, the apparatus was set-up again. McLean was hanged again.

Legends

The story of the man who was hanged twice has lived on in media coverage. It seems each new generation wants to hear the story.

The *Progressive Batavian* recounted the hanging in a Nov. 12, 1880 story:

> *On August 28th, 1807, over 73 years ago, James McLean was hanged in this village for the murder of Wm. Orr...He was arrested in Canandaigua, and brought to Batavia for trial. The gallows was erected at a point in the rear of where C.H. TURNER & Son's market now stands, and the stumps of the gallows posts, which, apparently, were made from a black ash tree cut in two parts, stood there, well preserved, for many years.*

The Man Who Was Hanged Twice

At the execution a shocking scene occurred, McLean being hung twice. The first time the rope broke, and a bed cord was procured from the house of Chauncey Keyes, which was doubled, and the execution proceeded. The murder created the most intense excitement throughout this region, and the hanging was witnessed by a large crowd composed by people from great distances who assembled to see the murder of Orr avenged. It was the all-absorbing topic of conversation at that time, and the story of the crime and the punishment was told and retold hundreds of times during the succeeding score of years.

Over forty years later, on February 28, 1926—in an article notable for its departure from journalistic form—a newspaper commemorated the event:

McLean was alleged to have remarked, when the hangman's rope broke, "As I killed two men, I deserve two hangings". Another version has him pleading that since he had been hanged, "he had already served his sentence".

Archibald McLaughlin, pioneer farmer, shambling along the newly built road that led south from Caledonia, on that spring day in 1807 little realized that shortly he was to play an unwelcome role in one of the most brutal murders in the annals of Western New York. Could he have seen what was to happen at his destination, it is doubtful he would have hummed a tingling Scottish melody as he moved along the highway.

McLaughlin's thoughts might well have been on the monumental task in which he had had a hand since he left his native heath in Scotland ten years or so before. But it is more likely that he was thinking of some matters of less moment than that. Nevertheless he could not fail to note all around him the evidences of the struggle that he had, with his fellow-pioneers, conducted during the five years preceding. In those five years, Caledonia had risen from the wilderness.

Caledonia had risen, and it still was rising, when McLaughlin started out on his fatal journey. As he stepped angularly along, he trod the new turned earth of a highway that still was under construction. Five years before, in 1802, the walk that he was taking would have been less pleasant, for he would have been stumbling through a dense forest. The hand of these few hardy Scots had worked wonders....

McLaughlin was not especially a leader in the new community but his figure stands out most clearly through the years in the meager records of what occurred on this spring day in 1807. He was a typical pioneer type. Had he, as he stepped along the highway, bothered, he might have identified the various log cabins he passed on the way. There were the crude homes of the McColls, the McLeans and the Orrs, along with that of his family.

Just what impelled McLaughlin to leave the settlement and start out on foot along the new highway cannot be determined at this late date, but in all probability he was bent on inspecting the work being done. He probably knew that James McLean, an ill-tempered resident of the colony, and William Orr were at work in the road just below the rude cabin home of Duncan McColl, three miles south of the settlement.

Had he stopped for a moment as he drew near the spot where the two were at work he would have seen the muscular form of James McLean, and beside him the person of William Orr. Some distance further on he would have seen Mrs. Duncan McColl, interestedly watching from the distance the workers, at the same time keeping an eye on her youngest child, then three years old. Donald McColl, her elder child, a likely lad of sixteen hardy summers, was at work clearing out some hazel brush through which the highway was to continue.

McLaughlin, if he stopped to look, saw McLean suddenly rise and gesticulated in an enraged frenzy at his fellow workman. Undoubtedly, the stroller started forward on a run when he saw McLean raise his ax above his head, threatening Orr. The fact remains that the blow crashed down before he could reach the scene. Orr fell dead to the ground, his skull cleft from the heavy broad ax in the hands of a powerful man.

Rushing forward, McLaughlin fell to his knees beside the murdered man. McLean, his mind crazed by the sight of the calamity that he had wrought, swung about and smote the kneeling McLaughlin with the bright blade. The heavy ax cut him to the heart.

So it was but the work of a moment, and two lives had been snuffed out…The horror of his acts swept over McLean as he found himself alone in the woods, and he plunged into the wilderness…It is said that during the time he was in jail, he was visited by a clergyman who found him a sincerely penitent man and who was able to convince him that a merciful God would forgive him. In that hope, he met his death. The story is told that the rope broke as McLean's weight fell. While another rope was being secured, McLean remarked that as he killed two men he deserved two hangings.

McLean was an uncle of Alexander McLean, for many years a member of the police force…Although a century and a quarter has passed, the old McColl homestead has been pointed out as haunted, and superstitious ones imagine that these Scots come back each spring in spirit and reenact this murder.[9]

Chapter 3
The Murder of William Lyman

At approximately 9:00 P.M., William Lyman closed up the office at the Rochester Railroad Company where he worked and set off down the street toward his home. Lyman, a devoted family man and diligent employee, was employed by the J.W. Hooker Mill as a purchasing agent, dealing in wheat commodities. In this capacity, Lyman frequently handled large cash transactions and as was his custom, carried a large bundle of cash home with him for the evening. It was to be deposited in the bank the following morning, on his way to work.

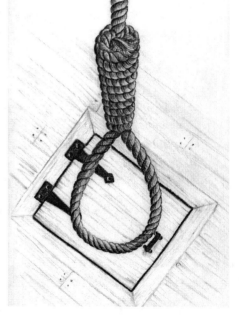

Lyman had apparently not noticed (or if he had, had apparently not been alarmed by) the man, it would later be reported, who had been seen loitering around outside the railroad office all day. Lyman took his customary path home, walking through the streets of his adopted city, Rochester. Born into a prominent colonial family in Massachusetts, Lyman had moved to

The Murder of William Lyman

Rochester in the early 1820s. As had so many others, he had been drawn by economic potential, and came to take work in the industry that was fueling much of that growth: The trade in foodstuffs and other natural resources along the Erie Canal.

As Lyman neared his home on Clinton Street, located a short distance from Hoodoo Corner, he took a shortcut into an open alley that would allow him easy access to his house. The alley was unlit. As Lyman took the last few paces toward his home, the man who had been following him all along made his move, creeping up behind Lyman and shooting once into the back of his head, killing him instantly.

It was October 20, 1837, and William Lyman, age thirty-seven and the father of four young children, had just become the first murder victim in Rochester history.

But it just so happened that Lyman and his attacker were not the only people in the area at the time. Thomas Dixon, nine years old, was also nearby. According to the witness statement he later gave to police, he was heading toward his own home on a course that took him by the Second Baptist Church, located at the intersection of Clinton and Main Streets. Dixon reported that he heard the 9 P.M. bell and a few minutes later, when he got to the fence by Franklin Street, he was "alarmed by the sounds of footsteps" nearby. He paused, then heard a shot and saw a flash as the gun discharged. Believing that he had witnessed a man shooting a dog that had been barking—and frightened by the man with the gun, who wore a "shiny hat" and who then "bent down" over something—Dixon turned and ran home.

Amanda Lyman also heard the gun discharge. She went to the window and drew back the curtain and looked out, but saw nothing. She also knew, she told the police, that something was wrong when her husband hadn't arrived home by 9:10 P.M. to take his evening tea. But neither Dixon nor Amanda Lyman took any further action that evening. The city went to sleep as usual, not yet knowing that one of its prominent, upstanding citizens had been murdered.

Early the next morning, when Dixon awoke, he made his way to the yard where he had seen the flash of light and heard the shot the night before. He expected to find the body of a dog, but was shocked to see "someone lying in the field," so he went home and told his father, and showed him "where the man was." Or such was the testimony that Dixon gave during the trial of the man who would eventually be convicted of Lyman's murder. It should be

The Middle Falls in Rochester. On the far bank is the Hooker Flour Mill where William Lyman was employed at the time of his murder.

noted, though, that Dixon's testimony at trial, and in the immediate aftermath of the event, was somewhat different. When he testified at the indictment proceedings, roughly a week after the murder, he claimed that upon discovering the body, he noticed that "a package wrapped in brown paper lay near the hat, close to where the blood showed that the victim had dropped when shot." Dixon "placed the package in the hat, and set the hat beside the head of the body." He then "told some other boys of the corpse, and they went to rouse the neighbors," before Dixon finally decided to go get his father.

Although the precise detail—whether Dixon touched the hat and the package or not (there was not yet any concept of scientific analysis of a crime scene, so the boy cannot be faulted for contaminating it) and then went to get his father or simply told some neighborhood boys about the body—isn't significant historically, it does point to one of the difficulties in reconstructing traumatic events, especially when they are historical episodes such as this. There are some discrepancies in the accounts of this crime in the sources, particularly between what a witness says early on, and then says later.

Nevertheless, the language of the participants in the trial—the lawyers, judge, witnesses—is remarkable: unique and rich, descriptive, and emotional. And thus we allow the participants to speak for themselves whenever possible.[10]

Outrage Unparalleled in Rochester—Assassination!

The Daily Advertiser, October 30, 1837

By 7 A.M., neighbors and passerby were gathering in the area just behind Lyman's house, to observe the body, lying face down, stiff and cold. There was a one-inch bullet wound behind Lyman's right ear. The location of blood and the marks on the ground suggested that Lyman's body had been dragged a few feet from where he initially fell. His outerwear had been removed, and his pockets had been turned inside out. Lyman's wallet and another small satchel were missing. Both of those were believed to contain money, estimated to be a few hundred paper dollars, and a few gold coins. The package that had been found lying near his hat was found to contain $5,000 in Connecticut River Banking Company money. The killer or killers had apparently missed it. Within minutes of the discovery, an alarm was issued. Word spread quickly through town and rewards for information about the murder were immediately posted.

Robert King, the sheriff of Monroe County, arrived quickly with a team of eleven men and took charge of the investigation. He wasted no time in interviewing Dixon, whose description of the "shiny hat" immediately became the most important clue. Only one kind of man wore a shiny cap—or a "glazed" cap, as it was also known—and that was a foreigner who worked on the canal or in the mills. It was well-known that these men congregated on the east side of State Street, which was a collection of nine-pin alleys, low saloons, and disorderly houses; i.e., brothels.

King immediately dispatched men to question people who lived in the area. A second piece of crucial information quickly emerged. It came from Hannah Chamberlain, a waitress who worked in a pub near State Street. She reported that upon getting off work the previous evening, "something caught my eye down on the first floor, where the tavern is." She noticed, she said, "three men sitting at a table with a pile of money between them. They were talking in loud whispers, and looking all around. The one who was doing most of the talking seemed pretty pleased with himself, because he ordered brandies all around." She had seen him there before, she noted, and she thought that he was called "Barron." And, she continued, "I don't know anything about him, except he wears one of those glazed caps."

Sheriff King later recalled:

> *It didn't take us long to locate the Barron house, as they were well-known. I spoke to Mrs. Margaret Barron, who said she had a son named Octavius. She didn't know his whereabouts, and had not seen him since yesterday. The young man, age 18, was not unknown to the police, or to the people of Rochester. He was French Canadian, a part-time barge worker, and a petty thief. It was common knowledge that he frequented the taverns and alleys of State Street, and that he usually lived with his mother in the Bowery, not far from where Lyman was murdered.*

Providentially, once Sheriff King had secured that crucial piece of information—that Barron had not been home the previous evening— he was "informed that someone at the train depot had reported a suspicious person lurking there, and as it was only a few blocks away, we went to investigate."

Sheriff King continued:

> *When we arrived at the depot, a Mr. Buckland from New York, who had just arrived on the 8:30 am train, said he had seen someone who had appeared in an unusual hurry, considering the time of day. When we began to search the area, we saw a man kneeling behind a wood pile. Stuck in this woodpile was a handkerchief, with bank notes rolled up inside. When we emptied the pockets of this person, we found more bank notes that seemed to match those in the handkerchief, as well as three gold coins. When questioned, the man said he was going*

The Murder of William Lyman

to Buffalo to look for a job. His name was Octavius Barron. I put the cuffs on him and took him to jail.

Further investigation soon enough determined the identities of the two men in the bar with Barron the previous evening: Leon Fluett and Thomas Bennet. They were quickly arrested as accomplices to the crime. Fewer than twelve hours after the murder, the perpetrator was in custody, and would never see freedom again. Barron was quickly and easily arraigned—the evidence against him was overwhelming—and he was sent to Sing-Sing Prison to await trial.

The Trial

Barron was returned to Monroe County just before his trial began on May 28, 1838. The murder and subsequent trial were the biggest spectacle in Rochester since the disappearance of Captain William Morgan nearly a decade before, and thus the subject of highly detailed newspaper coverage—including verbatim transcription of some witness testimony. The courthouse was packed to capacity with spectators anxious to learn every detail of the crime, and catch a glimpse of the killer, on each of the ten days of the trial.

The trial was presided over by Judge Charles Wentworth, a man known for his oratory, his no-nonsense approach to jurisprudence, and his strict adherence to the law. He had once convicted a man of lewdness for kissing his girlfriend in public.

The opposing lawyers were also well-known in the community, and well-respected for their legal abilities. Curiously, both were also well-known abolitionists. The defense counsel was particularly concerned that the civil rights of Octavius Barron, a French Canadian immigrant, be protected. The murder and ensuing publicity had seemed to release the simmering anger many townspeople felt over immigrants, particularly French Canadians, who were overwhelmingly Catholic. There was religious bigotry in the air. Such social tensions were entirely predictable in a city undergoing such rapid growth as Rochester—the population had doubled in just the previous decade. Thus, many French Canadian workers in the town felt generally—but especially during this period—that they were unwelcome residents of the city. And in addition to the issue of Barron's national origin and religion, there was the issue of his age. Barely eighteen at the time of the crime, there were some who hoped for—and many more who opposed—a death-penalty pardon on that basis.

The prosecutor, Ashley Sampson, lived in Pittsford, in a fine house on Main Street. The house still stands to this day, and still contains an original secret door, behind which he hid runaway slaves before they were taken further north, to escape across the river to Canada. Sampson made diligent use of his oratorical skills throughout the trial, as indicated in this excerpt from his opening statement:

> *Every moment's reflection adds to the horror of the deed. The murderer must have been a cool, deliberate villain. The whole bloody scene seems to bear the impress of cautious design, and we doubt not that when all of the facts are developed, it will be found to be the most diabolical offense to darken our fair corporation. The people will show that Octavius Barron hid in the shadows of Mr. Lyman's office on the evening of October 20 last, as he began his journey home...As the poor Mr. Lyman approached his abode on Clinton Place, Mr. Barron crept up behind him and viciously shot him in the head, killing him outright. Quickly taking what he found in Mr. Lyman's pockets, and neglecting to discover the much larger sum of money that Mr. Lyman was protecting under his hat, Barron then joined his friends to celebrate his new-found wealth. After a night of drinking and debauchery, Barron convinced his associates to bring his belongings to the railroad station, for his planned escape.*
>
> *We found Mr. Lyman's money on Barron. We will prove that others saw him following that night. We will prove his alibi to be nothing but lies. And we will prove without a doubt that Octavius Barron is the wanton and depraved killer of William Lyman. You must find him guilty!*

The Murder of William Lyman

The witness list included forty people, six of whom were able to place Barron in crucial locations on the night of the murder: Four who saw Barron loitering outside Lyman's office, and two who saw Barron following Lyman on his walk home that night.

Perhaps the most eagerly anticipated witness was one who had not seen Barron at all on the night of the murder: Margaret Barron, his mother. Under questioning, she refuted the alibi Octavius had given the police—that he was home, asleep at the time of the crime. Her testimony was steadfast; she stated outright that he hadn't spent the night at home. She also identified the handkerchief containing the dead man's money as belonging to her son.

Throughout the trial, Barron was demonized by the prosecutor and witnesses alike, referred to as a devil and miscreant. It was suggested time and again that Barron's path in life was already set—he was a petty thief, habitual gambler, drinker, and carouser—and there was no hope he would ever escape his criminal ways. Barron nonetheless stuck to his plea of not guilty.

The defense lawyer had little at his disposal with which to work. Barron owned and customarily wore a shiny glazed cap. His own mother refuted his alibi. There was no credible reason given for Barron to be in possession of Lyman's money and gold coins.

There were, however, three critical questions that were not answered by trial testimony: First, the role of Barron's accomplices, Fluett and Bennet. Second, the provenance and disposition of the murder weapon itself. And third, the whereabouts of Barron on the night of the murder, after he was seen by Chamberlain, the pub waitress, and before he was apprehended at the train station the next morning.

In any case, despite the unanswered questions, the trial of Octavius Barron concluded. The closing argument for the prosecution lasted three hours, while the closing argument for the defense lasted four hours. The judge's instructions to the jury took another three hours. In the end, the thirty-nine jurors needed just fifty minutes for their deliberations. Their verdict: Guilty!

The Sentence

Once the jury had given its verdict, the only significant question that remained in the minds of many was Barron's sentence. There was some hope—or fear, depending on one's perspective—that a death sentence might be avoided because of Lyman's age. But Judge Charles Wentworth quickly made clear, indicating at the very opening of his passing of sentence, that there would be no mercy from his Court. He said, speaking directly to Barron:

> *The evidence shows that you have long associated with the most vicious and depraved...That your companions were gamblers, blacklegs, and prostitutes, and that these habits and associations have prepared you for the commission of this last most fatal crime. Your heart is so effectively hardened that we dare not expect anything we may can reach or soften it. That can only be done by a power more than human.*

> *When you raised the weapon of death against Lyman, you doubtlessly supposed that no eye beheld your deed of blood, but the manner of this wonderful trial which has been made, shows that the All-seeing Eye was upon you, and saw your every movement. He has made it the occasion of showing His providence and His power. Before His tribunal you must be arraigned. The sentence of this court upon your case is that you be hung by the neck until you are dead.*

> *We must now add that the aggravated circumstances of your case forbid the hope of pardon or any mitigation of your punishment. You must now prepare for death. Your life has been worse than useless. We will hope that at least your death is of some profit to others, as a warning to deter them from a life of vice and crime.*

The Confession

As preparations for carrying out the sentence got underway, the story of Octavius Barron took the kind of twist that one sometimes sees, or hopes to see, in a Hollywood movie. Although the legal proceedings were concluded, it is perhaps fair to say that issues of justice and redemption remained. And they would be addressed in Barron's final hours.

On the eve of his execution, Barron was allowed visitors. The first was his mother, Margaret, who, not content simply to say good bye to her son, instead pleaded with him to confess, so that his soul would go to heaven. Observers claimed that Barron at first refused, still maintaining his innocence. But then, as his mother was leaving her son for the last time, and "with a decency that he had never before displayed," Barron apologized to his mother, and admitted that he had murdered William Lyman, and what is more, that he wished to formally confess his deed. By this, he meant in both religious and legal terms.

The sheriff and two clergymen were summoned, one Roman Catholic and the other Protestant. Barron then gave a confession in the presence of these men, and specifically to the Catholic priest, Reverend Bernard O'Reilly of St. Patrick's Church. Barron reportedly confessed in full, clearing the names of the men who had been charged as his accomplices, and accounting for the method by which he had secured and disposed of the murder weapon. Barron also said that he had thrown Lyman's still-missing satchel into the river. Finally, just hours before his death, Barron admitted to killing another man years before in a dispute over gambling. Barron allowed that his execution would be just punishment for that crime as well.

Barron then reportedly did his penance, praying in both French and Latin, and asked for God's forgiveness. When he was finished, Barron turned to the sheriff, and asked for one thing in return for the confession. He requested that upon his stepping onto the gallows, he "be hanged right away."

This seems at first glance an odd request. But the likely reasoning for the request lies in the nature of execution by hanging. It is arguably one of the most brutal methods for carrying out a death sentence. There are many variables for an executioner to consider when conduction an execution by hanging: The height and weight of the man, the length of the drop, and the precise placement of the rope around the neck. These factors are crucial in determining the length of time it takes a man to die, and the amount of pain he will suffer in the process.

The complications of death of by hanging were common knowledge in nineteenth-century America, as the method was widely used. The results were sometimes quite gruesome, depending on the skill, attention to detail, and conscientiousness of the executioner. In fact, the highly variable outcomes of death by hanging are the main reason it became gradually outlawed as a method of capital punishment in the United States during the twentieth century.

It seems that Barron was aware of these possibilities, and essentially made a request for the most humane death possible. In this period, the two most commonly used methods of hanging were known as the short drop and long drop. The short drop was the condemned man's worst fear. Commonly used prior to 1850, it usually involved a cart, horse, or stool, upon which the condemned was stood. Once the noose was around his neck, the support was removed. The resulting drop could be as little as a few inches, which meant that the prisoner slowly strangled to death. The weight of his body and his struggle worked to tighten the noose, which would eventually close off his airway and/or the carotid arteries, which supply blood to the brain. Not only could this be an excruciatingly slow death—strangulation often took ten to twenty minutes—it was often quite painful.

The long drop was developed as a more humane way to execute death sentences, and came into widespread use in the latter nineteenth century. Unlike the short drop, in which everyone fell roughly the same distance, in this method the person's body weight determined the distance of the drop, usually between six and eight feet. The method was also the best way to ensure that the individual's neck would be broken, resulting in instant death. There were, however, sometimes complications with this method as well—particularly, unintended decapitations. Nevertheless, the odds of a faster, less painful death were better with this method of hanging.

When Barron asked to be hanged "right away" in return for his confession, he was in effect asking that the long drop be employed, and perhaps that the executioner be carefully chosen as well. Barron was hoping for an executioner who would do his best to ensure that he not suffer needlessly.

The Execution

Given the overwhelming interest in the trial, and the anger and outrage of Rochester's citizens over the crime and its perpetrator, it is not surprising that many residents were hoping for a public execution. But the legislature of New York had three years previously outlawed them. Instead, the execution would be held indoors, on July 25, 1838, between the hours of one and two o'clock, on the first floor of the Monroe County Jail. There were forty-nine witnesses in attendance, including many public officials, physicians, judges, prison officers, and noble citizens of Rochester.

According to a newspaper account at the time, "Barron appeared on the first floor of the jail at 1:40 P.M., accompanied by the Sheriff and the two clergymen who were praying in Latin and in French. Barron wore a white roundabout, white pantaloons, and a ruffle shirt. His countenance betook

Photo of Octavius Barron's grave site. Barron is believed to have been the first person ever interred in Mount Hope Cemetery. Incredibly, twenty years later, William Lyman was re-buried in the same section of the cemetery.

great horror." But, witnesses agreed, "Barron stepped up onto the platform of his own accord and stood without trembling. He asked for the forgiveness of those he had injured, and also for the forgiveness of God."

The noose was placed around his neck and the supporting platform was removed, and "he died with little struggle, holding a Catholic cross in his right hand." Thus ends the ignominious life of Octavius Barron.

Barron was buried in the Public Grounds of Mount Hope cemetery, which was newly established during the summer of 1838. Barron's life was a bizarre series of improbable "firsts:" Rochester's first murderer and first person executed in the city, probably the first person ever hung using the "long-drop" method, and the first person interred in the newly-established cemetery. Today, Barron lies in an unmarked grave.

Chapter 4

The Assassination of Joseph Smith

Today, the town of Palmyra, in western New York, is a town of some 7,600 residents, which also includes the village of Palmyra, with nearly 3,500 inhabitants. Among the latter's claim to fame is that it is the only place in the United States in which four churches at a four-corner intersection face each

other. It is perhaps a fitting distinction for the place where the first Book of Mormon was printed, in 1830, by the publisher E.B. Grandin. The area thus was the center of one of the most remarkable religious developments of the early nineteenth century. The birth of a new, wholly American religion, one that is today the fastest growing church on earth: The Church of Jesus Christ of Latter-day Saints.

Joseph Smith (1805–1844) was born in Vermont, to a migrant farming couple. The Smiths, by all accounts, had difficulties during Joseph's childhood. They moved frequently, as a consequence of both crop failures and ill-fated business ventures. During the winter of Joseph's eighth year, his leg became dangerously infected. Some doctors reportedly advised amputation, but the family refused. Smith underwent a successful operation to remove part of his shin bone (without anesthesia or the then-most-commonly used tranquilizer, whiskey.) He eventually recovered, although he used crutches for several years and limped for the rest of his life.

The family resumed its transient lifestyle, moving from town to town, looking for work. In 1816 or 1817 (the evidence is unclear), the Smith family was "warned out of" the town in Vermont in which they lived. This was a commonly-used method in New England, a way that communities pressured "outsiders" to settle elsewhere, and can probably be traced to the family's financial difficulties. The family then left New England, moving to the village of Palmyra. For three years, the father and elder sons worked odd jobs and squatted in a log home until they were able to obtain a mortgage for a hundred-acre farm in the nearby town of Manchester.

The Smith family does not appear to have been extraordinarily religious. There is no evidence that they regularly attended church, but Joseph did participate in some church events. There is some conflicting evidence about whether he regularly read the Bible as a child, though his mother seemed to indicate that he did not do so until his late teens. With his family, he took part in religious folk magic, which was then a common practice but one that many Christian clergymen condemned. Like many people in that era, the family believed in Christian mysticism, and both of Joseph's parents and his maternal grandfather had visions and dreams that they believed communicated messages from God.

Smith's own first vision occurred in the spring, during a walk in the woods. It was, he later said, the first time that he attempted to pray. He kneeled, he said, and: "began to offer up the desires of my heart to God." The account continues:

> *I had scarcely done so, when immediately I was seized upon by some power which entirely overcame me, and had such an astonishing influence over me as to bind my tongue so that I could not speak. Thick darkness gathered around me, and it seemed to me for a time as if I were doomed to sudden destruction. But, exerting all my powers to call upon God to deliver me out of the power of this enemy which had seized upon me, and at the very moment when I was ready to sink*

into despair and abandon myself to destruction—not to an imaginary ruin, but to the power of some actual being from the unseen world, who had such marvelous power as I had never before felt in any being—just at this moment of great alarm, I saw a pillar of light exactly over my head, above the brightness of the sun, which descended gradually until it fell upon me...It no sooner appeared than I found myself delivered from the enemy which held me bound.

Though this vision might have had an immediate and profound effect on Smith, it was some time before it became the guiding force of his life.

HILL CUMORAH WHERE THE BOOK OF MORMON WAS FOUND   JOSEPH SMITH FARM, PALMYRA, N.Y.

A view of Hill Cumorah located in Palmyra, New York. This spot is considered to be the place where the Angel Moroni buried a set of gold plates later found by Joseph Smith which he then translated into the Book of Mormon.

Smith had very little formal schooling, and filled his time by working on his father's farm, hunting, fishing, taking odds jobs, and pursuing small business ventures, e.g., selling cake and beer at public events. Smith was described

The Grandin Print Shop where the Book of Mormon was originally printed. When Smith delivered the manuscript it had been written as a 543 page, one sentence document with no punctuation. It took three months to edit.

by contemporaries as quiet, even taciturn, and though good-natured, he wasn't given to laughing. In 1822, the Smiths began building a frame house located on the property that they owned. In November, 1823, Joseph's older brother Alvin died. By 1825, the Smiths were unable to make their final mortgage payment, and the house and farm were foreclosed on. Desperate, the family persuaded a neighbor, Lemuel Durfee, to buy the farm, and they rented it back from him.

One of the ways the Smith family supplemented its meager farm income was by treasure-digging. This was a relatively common activity in this period. Joseph, in particular, claimed a special ability to use "seer" stones for locating lost items and buried treasure. He'd put a stone in a white stovepipe hat and then apparently receive information about the location of items in reflections given off by the stone. Folklore held that a treasure-seeker maintained his powers by preserving sexual purity, and this seems to have had a profound effect on Smith.

One night in 1823, perhaps while praying to be purified from a sexual sin, Smith said he was visited by an angel named Moroni. The angel revealed that there was a cache of items hidden in a nearby hill named Cumorah. The cache included a buried book made of golden plates, a breastplate, and a set of silver spectacles with lenses composed of seer stones. Smith later reported that he attempted to remove the golden plates the next morning, but that was unable to do so because the angel struck him down with force, saying that the tablets could only be removed when Smith was accompanied to Cumorah by the "right person."

The Assassination of Joseph Smith

Over the next few years, Smith made annual visits to Cumorah, but returned each time without the golden plates, because the angel was dissatisfied in some way by the people he had with him. Smith would later say that his

Room where Joseph Smith translated the Book of Mormon. His wife was amazed he could work all day in the fields and then take up precisely where he had left off the night before".

brother Alvin was in fact the "right person" but by the time Joseph figured that out, Alvin had died. Meanwhile, Smith continued to travel western New York and Pennsylvania as a treasure hunter. He was arrested and tried in 1826 as a "disorderly person" for these activities. In 1827, he met a young woman named Emma Hale. They fell in love and then eloped, because her parents disapproved of the match.

Believing that Emma would satisfy the angel as the "right person," Smith went with her to Cumorah on September 22, 1827. This time, he successfully retrieved the plates and placed them in a locked chest. He refused to allow anyone, including his family, to view the plates directly, saying that the angel had commanded him not to show the plates, but only to publish a translation of them. Smith reportedly kept the plates in a chest under the hearth in his parents' home, then later moved them under the floor boards of his parents' old log home nearby. He also reported that at one point, he took the plates out of the chest, left the empty chest under the floor boards, and hid the plates in a barrel of flax. It appears that Smith was particularly concerned about the safety of the plates because he was involved a dispute with other treasure-hunters, who accused him of double-crossing them and taking for himself what was rightly joint property. Some dozen of them ransacked his hiding places, looking for stolen loot, and/or the golden plates. Smith is said to have realized that he could not accomplish the translation of the golden plates in Palmyra. He took a loan of $50 from a neighbor, paid his debts in Palmyra, and then moved with his wife to Harmony Township, Pennsylvania.

The neighbor might be counted as the first of Smith's religious followers. The man had agreed to the loan after hefting the chest said to contain the plates, and he professed a belief in Smith's mission. Smith began to build a following as news of the golden plates spread. The plates, Smith said, described the religious history of American indigenous peoples. In March of 1830, Smith published a translation from the "reformed Egyptian" of the golden plates, titled *The Book of Mormon: An Account Written by the Hand of Mormon upon Plates Taken from the Plates of Nephi*. The Book of Mormon is divided into smaller books, titled after individuals named as primary authors and, in most versions, divided into chapters and verses. The English is very similar to the early modern English style of the King James Bible. The original manuscript reportedly ran to some 532 pages, and was one long sentence. It took the editor three months to punctuate it.

In 1830, Smith organized the first church of Latter-day Saints, claiming it was a restoration of the true church of Jesus Christ, from which other churches had strayed, due to a Great Apostasy. Smith also left the region that year, taking the majority of his church members to Kirtland, Ohio. He sent another group to Jackson County, Missouri, in an attempt to establish a city of Zion there, as the biblical New Jerusalem. But Smith's plans for Zion were repeatedly frustrated. In 1833, Missouri settlers expelled the Latter-day Saints from Jackson County, and Smith's paramilitary campaign to redeem the area was unsuccessful. Smith turned his attention to Kirtland, and undertook the construction of an expensive temple there. But in early 1838, after a financial scandal effectively caused the collapse of the church there, Smith fled an arrest warrant, and joined those of his followers who remained in Missouri. When many of the Kirtland Saints followed him to Missouri, tensions escalated with non-LDS settlers. Amidst open warfare, Smith was jailed for four months. The Saints were then expelled from Missouri by Governor Lilburn L. Boggs.

In 1839, Smith and his followers settled in Nauvoo, Illinois. Taking a lesson from previous instances in which the presence of the Mormons became unacceptable to residents of an area, Smith sought to ground the church presence in secular authority as well. He became the mayor of the town, and commander of the Nauvoo Legion, a sizeable branch of the Illinois militia. He also directed the construction of a second temple. Smith consolidated his authority and introduced changes into the church, formally ratified in 1843. These doctrines included "plural marriage, the eternal progression of man toward godhood, eternalizing of the marriage covenant, the endowment ceremony, and the political kingdom of God with its secret Council of Fifty."[11] The formalization of these matters began a schism in the church that would widen over time, and as Smith became involved in politics.

In 1844, Smith declared his candidacy for the presidency of the United States.[12] He campaigned as General Joseph Smith (given that he was a Lieutenant General of the Nauvoo Legion by state and federal appointment), and his central campaign issue was power of the federal government to quell violence and preserve civil order in the states when the states failed to do so. Smith thus took aim at Article IV of the Constitution, which declares that federal troops may enter a state only under request from the governor. Smith's position grew out of his experience with Missouri Governor Boggs, and the response of federal authorities. In November 1839, in the midst of his troubles in Missouri, Smith met with President Martin Van Buren and pleaded the LDS case, but the president was unmoved. Some four months later, after considerable political effort to enlist politic support by church leaders in Washington, Van Buren gave his final word on the issue, saying, "Your cause is just, but I can do nothing for you. If I take up for you I shall lose the vote of Missouri." For Smith, it was a crucial turning point.

In late 1843, as the presidential election cycle was beginning, Smith wrote to the leading candidates—including John C. Calhoun, Lewis Cass, Richard M. Johnson, Henry Clay, and Martin Van Buren—and asked how they would handle the persecution of the Mormons. Receiving no satisfactory responses, Smith called a meeting in the mayor's office at Nauvoo on January 29, 1844. Church leaders—including the quorum of the Twelve Apostles—and other civil leaders (who were also church members), unanimously decided that Smith would run for president as an independent, with the central plank that it was the duty of the federal government to protect the right of all citizens. Soon, Smith would go so far as to prescribe capital punishment for presidents who didn't do so. He said, "The Constitution should contain a provision that every officer of the government who should neglect or refuse to extend the protection guaranteed in the Constitution should be subject to capital punishment; and then the president of the United States would not say, "'Your cause is just, but I can do nothing for you'..."

Soon the campaign drew up a pamphlet, *General Smith's Views of the Powers and Policy of the Government of the United States*, which stated his views on the issues of the day. Fifteen hundred copies were printed and sent to

Joseph Smith (1805-1844) "I don't blame anyone for not believing my history. If I had not experienced what I have, I would not have believed it myself."

political leaders and newspapers all over the country. The platform covered a broad range of topics. Smith was anti-slavery, though he did not believe that simple abolition was the answer. His plan was novel in that it required the government to "buy" the freedom of slaves through the sale of land in the West. It went hand-in-glove with another platform point: Reducing not only the pay of Congressmen, but the number of representatives in Congress, significantly. His platform was comprehensive, if quirky and perhaps unexpected, if one assumes that he would in the modern era be a conservative. He supported, for instance, a National Bank. He supported penal reform (about which he said, "Let penitentiaries be turned into seminaries of learning,"), abolishing courts-martial for military desertion, and the end of debtors' prisons. He wanted to immediately annex the Oregon Territory and hoped to expand the union in consultation with Native Americans; and even to expand the union to Mexico and Canada.[13]

By April 1844, tensions were rising on both the secular and religious fronts. Smith had created a campaign organization that resembled that of the church; that is, sending out "missionaries" to campaign for him across the country. Though some attempt was made to separate the political campaign from church activity, the lines were blurred. His surrogates were sometimes met with violence at campaign events, and a movement against him was gaining momentum. One political enemy, a Dr. Southwick of Illinois, reportedly said that if Smith "did not get into the Presidential chair this election, he would be sure to the next time; and if Illinois and Missouri would join together and kill him, they would not be brought to justice for it." Meanwhile, some LDS members were leaving the church or being forced out. Several key members—including Smith's second counselor and one of the presidents of the Nauvoo Stake and several business and professional people—were excommunicated. They then purchased a printing press and began publishing a newspaper, *The Nauvoo Expositor.* The paper made a number of charges against Smith: That he was a tyrant and that he had introduced into the church doctrine and practices which were contrary to the original teachings of the church. On June 7, 1844, they publicly exposed the practice of polygamy within the church, calling it "whoredoms and abominations," and accused Smith of being behind it.[14] The stage was now set for the last act of Smith's life.

The Nauvoo Expositor subsequently published another article suggesting that Smith was going to address the concerns, and that Smith intended to repeal the city charter, so that the city might be governed in accordance with principles of the separation of church and state. The following morning and the Monday thereafter, the city council and Mayor Joseph Smith met to consider the problem. They then termed the charges against Smith a threat to the peace and security of the city, and used their power to declare the newspaper a "nuisance." Thus, Smith in effect declared martial law in the city. The government of the state of Illinois then got involved, accusing Smith of treason. He was arrested and jailed.

But before a trial could be held, on the afternoon of June 27, 1844, a mob of about 200 armed men stormed the jail, seeking Smith. He tried to defend himself with a small pistol that had been smuggled in to him, to no avail. Smith ran out of ammunition just as some of the men broke into the cell. Smith turned, to make his way toward the window, to jump, and was shot twice in the back. He was hit a third time, in the chest, by a bullet fired from a musket on the ground outside. His body fell out of the window. Some accounts suggest that Smith was alive when he hit the ground, and was abused by the crowd—perhaps even propped against a wall and executed—though the best evidence suggests he was in fact dead when his body hit the ground, and that his body was then mutilated by the crowd.

There is debate today whether Smith's killing can properly be called a political execution. In any case, while it was the end of Joseph Smith's life, it was the beginning of a new chapter for the Church of Jesus Christ of Latter-day Saints. Two years later, Brigham Young began the Mormon Exodus to Utah.

Chapter 5

The High Falls Murder

While today Rochester's Brown's Race Neighborhood is being revitalized—an up-and-coming entertainment area—in the nineteenth century it was an area of mills and factories. It is adjacent to the Genesee Gorge, which includes the ninety-six-feet-tall High Falls, the scene of a notorious murder. The murder of Charles Littles there in December 1857, gave rise to the most sensational murder trial in nineteenth-century Rochester. Marion Ira Stout was charged with the murder of his brother-in-law. During the trial, the subject of incest would play a large role. As one student of the case, put it:

For most of 1858, citizens were talking about Ira Stout and his sister, Sarah Littles. The unusual brother/sister relationship and family history added high drama and sordid detail to the

murder trial. In keeping with Victorian taste for the fantastic and bizarre, the newspapers had a field day covering the story. Detailed transcripts of the testimony were published daily. Several times, both newspapers in town had to publish extra copies just to keep up with public demand.[15]

In 1852, the Stout family moved to Rochester from Pennsylvania and, until the time of the murder, led a quiet existence. Eli Stout, Ira's older brother and head of the family, lived with his mother Margaret, his wife Jane, his younger sister Sarah and her husband Charles, in a house at 75 Monroe Street (now Monroe Avenue.) Margaret Stout often told friends and neighbors that her husband had abandoned the family and she was unsure of his whereabouts. But the truth was rather different. Members of the Stout family were often in trouble with the law. Orange Stout, Margaret's husband, was a member of a gang of forgers and counterfeiters. Both husband and wife had been previously

View of the Browns Race section of Rochester. During the nineteenth century Rochester had become one of the country's fastest growing cities. By 1860 Rochester was larger than Chicago.

arrested for passing counterfeit money. At the time of his son's murder trial, Orange Stout was serving a seven-and-a-half-year sentence in Auburn State Prison for his part in robbing and burning down a retail store in Pennsylvania.

In fact, Ira Stout (he used his middle name rather than his given name of Marion) had admitted participation in the crime and he'd served a four-and-a-half-year sentence. When he was released from prison in August 1858, he settled with his family in Rochester. Stout soon realized that marriage between his sister Sarah and her husband Charles was rocky. Littles, twenty-five years old, was a lawyer who dealt in insurance claims and was suspected of many shady business practices. He was known to be philanderer, and was also known to always carry a knife.

Sarah apparently became depressed and looked to her brother for emotional support. It was claimed at trial that she blamed all of problems on her husband, was unfaithful to him, and even considered moving west to escape from him. But, it was said, Ira suggested that "if Littles should some time be put out of the way, there would be no need of her going west to get rid of him."[16]

Ira had his own reasons to dislike and fear his brother-in-law. Only his own family and Littles knew of Ira's recent imprisonment. It was argued, in the newspapers at any rate, that Ira worried that Charles might destroy his standing by making this knowledge public. As one local historian put it:

> Stout...hoped to...start a new life. In Rochester, he enrolled in a local mercantile college. His days were spent studying shorthand and business math. At night, he studied law and brushed up on his already considerable knowledge of Latin, French, and classical literature. Eminently likeable, he soon made many friends and often acted as tutor to his fellow students. It was Ira's plan to continue his career in the mercantile business, which had been cut short by his brush with the law.[17]

Ira thus first sought to establish a friendship with Littles, calling frequently at his office. The two men were often seen playing pool together. But Stout couldn't ignore the way Littles treated Sarah, to whom Ira was very close. Perhaps too close as it turned out. Charles and Sarah had tumultuous relationships, as is clear in her testimony at trial.

I came home in October, he followed in December; he came to the house and told Eli that he had not used me right; he cried and promised to reform; I consented to live with him. In about two months he began to do as before; he was sick of a venereal disease, and I had to wait upon him; I then lived with my mother on Water Street; I continued to live with him till last spring; he was sick when I refused to live with him; it was a new sickness of the same disease; when he used to go away at night, he would tell me that he was going to the Niagara House to sleep with Lola Montez, or something like that. I did not believe it until I found it written in his diary; Lola

The High Falls in Rochester. It was here that Ira Stout murdered his brother-in-law, Charles Littles. The allegations were that Stout was having an affair with his sister and Littles was threatening to expose the relationship.

Montez was Ann Loder Gascoigne. I have since been with my mother; Littles did not provide for me; I once told him that he had got to do something to support me; he said that I could go and live with his mother as long as I was a mind to; there was no difficulty between us in consequence of my personal health; never had an altercation with him in presence of any of these women; I had recently told him that if he would do what was right, I would live with him in the spring. A week ago Saturday night I went to Mrs. Cunington's (boarding house) and staid all night; Littles came to Mrs. C's drunk, and wanted me to

*go home; I refused to go. He took out some money and threw
it down then drew his dirk knife and threw it against the wall
saying, that he did not fear God, man or the devil...[18]"*

Eventually, Stout was enraged by the way Sarah was treated—and/or
feared exposure of his own history and perhaps of his unnatural relationship
with Sarah — and vowed to do away with Littles.

The Crime

A few days before the murder took place, a man named Newhafer was walking
over the Andrews Street Bridge, which was being repaired at the time. He
slipped and fell into the Genesee River and was carried over the High Falls to
his death. The incident gave Stout the idea and the plan for the murder seemed
simple. Late at night, Stout would lure Littles to Falls Field, on the north side
of High Falls, on the false pretext that Sarah was going to meet another man.
Once there, Stout would hit Littles on the head with a hammer and throw him
into the gorge, allowing the strong current to sweep his body down river and
into the lake. Unfortunately for Stout, everything went horribly wrong.

A blow-by-blow account of that night was given by William F. Peck, a
local historian.

> *Littles was of a jealous disposition, which enabled Stout to
> convince him that his wife had an appointment at Falls Field
> for the evening of December 19, and the two men went to the
> spot on that night. Sarah, who was dominated by her brother,
> preceded them a little, so as to lure her husband to his doom.*
>
> *That came soon enough, for when they got near the edge of the
> bank, Ira struck his victim a sudden blow with an iron mallet,
> smashing the skull and producing death instantly. Stout then
> threw the body over the precipice, supposing that it would
> fall into the river and be swept into the lake before sunrise,
> but instead of that it landed on a projecting ledge thirty feet
> below the upper level. Perceiving that there had been some*

failure in the matter, Ira started to go down a narrow path that led sideways along the cliff, but in the darkness he missed his footing and fell headlong, breaking his left arm in the descent and landing beside the corpse. Summoning all his remaining strength he was just able to push the body over the bank, when he sank in a dead faint.

On recovering…he called to his sister, who was still above, to come and help him. When she started to do so, the bushes to which she clung gave way; she stumbled, broke her left wrist, and fell beside her prostrate brother. But it would not do to remain there, wretched as was their plight. So, after searching in vain for Ira's spectacles, which they had to leave behind them, but taking with them the fatal mallet, they scrambled slowly and painfully up the bank and made their way laboriously to their home on Monroe Street.

The first thing was to remove all obvious traces of the crime; the mallet was hidden away on the premises so carefully that it was not found till after the trial, and the blood stains were as far as possible washed away from their clothes…Both were able to bear without manifestation the pain of their wounds, but the swelling and the inflammation of Ira's arm increased so rapidly that the result might have been fatal if surgical aid had not been summoned, dangerous as that step was. So Dr. Rapalje and Dr. Whitebeck were called in at a late hour of the night, the limb was set and bandaged, Sarah not mentioning her own injury, and then the household waited for the dawn and for what might come after.

Stout had also misjudged the outcome of the Newhafer accident, because teams were still searching for the unfortunate man's body. That search took them directly where Stout did not want them to go. Peck continues:

The Jewish congregation of which Newhafer was a member offered a large reward for the recovery of his body, stimulated by which a number of persons engaged in the search and early on the morning of the 20ᵗʰ they went down the path which Ira and his sister had trodden the night before. Descending to its foot they found not the object of their search, but the corpse of Littles, which had been thrown back by the rushing water into a shallow eddy, where it remained.

It took not long to identify the remains, and within an hour the officers, armed with a warrant, went to the house on Monroe [A]venue, and there the evidence of guilt confronted them almost at once. Incredible as it may seem, Sarah, misled by her evil genius, had neglected to remove from her cloak and even from her hair the burrs of the yellow burdock that had clung to her in her frightful fall and that were afterward shown to be similar to those that grew in the fatal field.

The culprits were taken at once to the police office, where the coroner was already; a jury was immediately summoned, although it was Sunday, and the inquest proceeded through that whole day, late into the night and for the three days and evenings following. It was, practically, the trial, the subsequent proceedings before the grand and petty juries bringing out little more testimony than had been already produced.[19]

Coroner's Inquest

The coroner's inquest began the day after the mangled body of Charles Littles was found. The gruesome scene of the crime was described at the inquest, and details were carried in newspapers. The Rochester *Democrat and American* wrote:

Coroner Quinn explained that the head struck a bank of stone and gravel, where a piece of the skull and a pair of spectacles were found. From that point the body fell further down upon a flat stone, and then again to within a few feet of the water, where there was a pool of blood. From thence it was apparently dragged into the water, where it was found.

A struggle appears to have taken place. Found at the scene was part of a lady's victorine, an arm from a common wooden office chair, and prints of boots in the blood and soft earth. The body was found in the water, and had not floated from the place where thrown in....[20]

The victorine, a small cape commonly worn by women in the nineteenth century, was shown to have belonged to Sarah Littles. The arm from an office chair belonged to Stout. He had brought it with him to use as a weapon.

All members of the Stout family were immediately arrested and held in jail for questioning. In spite of the fact that Stout had confessed the murder to his family members before the arrest, all of them denied any involvement in the crime. The newspapers remarked on the family's relaxed attitude toward losing a member to violent death, and especially the nonchalance of Sarah. One journalist noted, "While Mrs. Littles was under examination, she evinced the utmost composure, although the surgeons were engaged within a few feet in dissecting the mutilated remains of her husband, and the horrid sound of the saw, severing the skull grated upon the ear. The examination of her broken wrist scarcely made her wince, although the pain must have been severe."

At the inquest, several family members testified to the unusual relationship between Stout and his sister, Sarah. As the newspapers reported breathlessly, Ira and Sarah were often seen together in the same bed in a state of undress. Several family members testified to that fact. In testimony, Eli Stout's wife, Jane, said that it had witnessed it, recently.

Two or three weeks ago; the last time was on Sunday morning; he got up in the morning, and it was cold, and he went and got into bed with Sarah; they got up, both of them, that Sunday morning; I couldn't give any guess as to the time they lay; he was undressed at the time I think. She was also undressed; did not go to the bed and look, after they were in bed; all I know is, that when Charley was not there and Ira was up late writing, he would lie in her bed; they were undressed, and the bed clothes on them, when I have seen them lying together; it was generally when we went that they would go to bed

together; they did not make it a practice of sleeping together...
these facts were known to the rest of the family.

The prosecutor asked probed further, asking who else in the household knew. Jane said both Stout's mother and Charles knew, saying of the latter that he, "He came in on Sunday morning and found them in bed together." Of the former, she said:

> *His mother would say that she should think he would be*
> *ashamed—in a joking way. He said it was nobody's business,*
> *it was his own sister. She replied she would tell him that if*
> *it was known, some might make something of it. He replied,*
> *'Then let them make it.'* [21]

The inquest continued into the New Year, when Stout was finally indicted for the murder of Littles. Sarah , her mother Margaret Stout, and Ira's younger brother Charley were named as accessories to murder. All of them remained in jail, awaiting trial, which was scheduled to begin in April.

The Trial

Most of the evidence in the case was adduced at the coroner's inquest and it wasn't expected there would be much new to learn at trial. Nevertheless, as Rochester's citizens anxiously awaited the trial, they continued to follow the case avidly. The Stouts, locked away in the city jail, were considered celebrities. On March 16, 1858, the *Union and Advertiser* wrote:

> *The common thieves, and those charged with forgery, perjury,*
> *and like offenses, are altogether unnoticed in the place where*
> *Ira Stout [is] imprisoned....Stout appeared to be in about*
> *the same even temper which has characterized him since his*
> *arrest...He assures us that we have published much in regard*
> *to his case which is absurd, although he has not read what*
> *has been published, but has been told of it by others...Mrs.*
> *Littles expresses regret that the rules of the jail prohibited*

her from reading the daily papers, or other newspapers...
Margaret Stout...we should infer from her deportment that
restraint was quite irksome to her as to any of the family...
Charley Stout, the boy...had before him a large pile of books
including the Bible and Shakespeare. He is a lad of more
than ordinary intelligence, and if trained to usefulness, might
become a valuable citizen; but under opposite influences
may be anything else...The jail is now much frequented by
citizens and strangers, led by curiosity....[22]

Ira Stout's trial began in April 1858 and lasted only a week. On April 24, the jury rendered a unanimous verdict of guilty and sentenced him to hang on June 18. But his lawyers immediately appealed the verdict. Shortly thereafter, Sarah Littles was tried for manslaughter and was convicted in the second degree. She was sentenced to a seven-year term in Sing Sing.

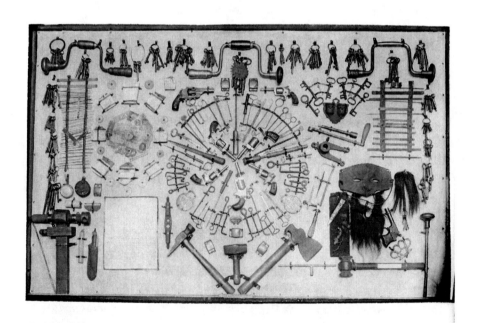

Weapons and tools collected by the police department. They include keys, guns and hatchets and other miscellaneous items used in crimes. The hammer at the lower right was used by Ira Stout to kill his brother-in-law

The High Falls Murder

Post-trial Developments

Stout's lawyer, John Pomeroy, believed Ira had not received a fair trial. It was leaked to the press that some of the jurors on the case had formed an opinion as to Stout's guilt before the trial had even begun. As a result, the judge granted a stay of execution. A motion for a new trial was scheduled to be argued in September. Stout spent the months in jail, giving rise to perhaps the oddest aspect of this case. Every day Stout entertained a multitude of visitors, many of them women. Many considered him an unjustly imprisoned hero, a victim of his parent's bad influence and a defender of his sister's honor. Many women were charmed and dazzled by him. The description given by the *Union and Advertiser*, however, doesn't suggest that he was an appealing character.

> *In personal appearance Stout had little to prepossess, although it is said a number of soft young ladies were struck with admiration on seeing him in court. He was tall, very slim, and walked erect. His hair and complexion were rather dark, his cheekbones high, nose rather long, and the general cast of his countenance is best expressed by those who said he had 'the look of an Indian.' His head was small, and he wore his hair long, which gave him a boyish appearance. His dark eyes were never at rest and were constantly seeking some new object. He had nothing like frankness in his countenance, but his expression was the reverse, and we may add that those who knew him best agree that the face was in his case a true index to his character.*[23]

While Stout waited for his case to proceed through the system, he engaged in what would today be called a public relations campaign on his own behalf. He was an avid letter writer, and many of his letters were published in the press. On May 4, 1858, Stout sent a letter to the editor of the *Rochester American*. The newspaper printed the letter, which was then picked up and widely reprinted in newspapers across the country. It read:

> *The trial is past. It is these terrific ordeals that either sweep the immortal mind from its proud throne, and crush it in the dust,*

57

or else call forth its vast energies to meet the killing storm, with a firmness which nothing can overturn. I arose to receive that verdict and sentence with a cool, determined resolution to stand unmoved, though it 'wrung the life blood from the heart.' There was no visible emotion to show the volcano boiling within, and the immense audience failed to perceive that the passionless exterior simply concealed an internal agony, of which no mortal man can form a conception. It was a terrible illustration how much a man may bear when supported by all the philosophy and self-control he possessed. To a young man, the startling word—death—terminates all his brilliant hopes and ambition, all his powerful attachments to earth; and not only his but the love, hope and interest of others, must slowly fade away.

I wish to speak of Littles, but I can hardly find it in my heart to make war upon the dead. Bad as he was, I bitterly regret his death; but the dead past can never be recalled. His connection with the family made me his friend and defender, and I acted toward him like a man and a brother. I thought his youth and inexperience 'would cover a multitude of sins': and though his conduct had been outrageous, yet he was more worthy of being pitied and assisted than condemned and avoided. In our first interview, he rehearsed to me the wretched drama of his life, and perhaps I am better acquainted with him than anyone; but I find it difficult to speak of him, simply because I feel no disposition to pen a record of disease and degradation. When he married Sarah she was mild and beautiful, pure and innocent, unskilled in the follies and flatteries of the world, and if placed under the control of a man of sense, she might have been molded into a model domestic beauty. God alone knows what she has suffered from this unhappy union.

Littles would return from his drunken orgies, and without the slightest cause abuse a woman he had sacredly sworn to love and protect, in the most brutal and disgusting manner. The old Rochester jail contains the final result of his inhuman conduct. If she and mother and little Charley were discharged tomorrow, it would be a just and honorable proceedings, and bitter as it is, I am ready to offer up my life as a ransom for their liberty. That I felt a brother's sympathy for Sarah, in regard to her wrongs, is too true. That my heart sometimes burst with indignation is equally true. And if there is a spirited brother in Christendom, who will stand passively by and see his sister abused, he out to be cared into cubic inches and fed to the dogs. My attachment to Sarah is simply a brother's love—the purest and holiest man can conceived. She possesses the faults and frailties of a woman; but no matter whether right or wrong, she is still my sister, and it is my sacred duty to defend her, as long as the power of action remains.

I do say most decidedly, a man who will abuse a pure and beautiful woman—a man who will strikes her—I say from the bottom of my heart, he is not fit to live. I know, as the district attorney would say, this is showing motive, pretty strongly: but while I see how much circumstances are against me, I will say, it is purely impossible for me to fight or injure anyone unless placed in a desperate position, where reason and self-control are suspended. My future hopes were too bright (and other hopes than mine rested on my actions,) my judgment and resolution were too strong, and I understood my situation too well, to engage in a transaction which would involve me in difficulty, unless I became the victim of an accident. Perhaps the public may shortly be informed of that most singular combination of circumstances that led to that unhappy collision which not only sent Littles to a horrible death but I fear he will drag another after him, who, I do believe, deserves a better fate. There is power for usefulness in me, if I only have an opportunity for development, and I appeal to the heart of each reader, if he does not fairly and candidly think I might be put to a better use than hanging. I do not wish to show a cowardly tenacity for life, but I consider it my right and duty to live as long as I can.

From the time I entered the city of Rochester up to this terrible accident, my course was onward and upward. I knew that my reputation must be raised on supported by my own industry and ability, and my days and nights were spent I the most laborious study, and in trying to elevate myself in the estimation of sensible men and women.

I ask those who visit me to speak to me as they would to a son or brother; and above all, to remember me and mine when bowed before the Throne of Mercy, and pray that we may meet in that bright world where care and sorrow never come.[24]

And Stout was the recipient of many letters as well, some from prominent citizens. Judge Charles P. Avery, who had sat on the bench for Stout's trial in Pennsylvania, wrote to him:

I pray you forget the past, and all bitterness connected with it as far as in you it lies and, in so doing, call to your aid that strength and light which come from above. A fine writer has said forcibly and beautifully, 'Look not mournfully into the past. It comes not back again. Wisely improve the present. It is thine.

If you but cast aside that self-reliant strength which seems so far to have borne you forward in life, you will be happier, better, and believe me, stronger in the humility and weakness of a little child than in the cool nerve and unchastened power of your manhood.

Stout replied:

When I think of my present situation, and what it might have been, the reflection is bitter-bitter and withering. Who is responsible for my life? Who shall answer for my death?

Had I been in my youth directed in the path of rectitude and honor, who will attempt to say that I might not have been at this minute, legislating in the halls of a State house or engaged in the purer and holier cause of religion, instead of dying by inches condemned in a cell. But I have no reproaches to make. God forbid, I could be guilty of making any bitter flings at those whom I am bound to regard with the purest reverence and affection.

I have often bowed before the unsullied greatness and goodness of your character, and I have at times been strongly impressed with the idea that perhaps I might someday be as much beloved and respected as you...

As Stout's letters were published in newspapers, many responded favorably to his claim that he would be a useful member of society, if given the chance. In September 1858, the motion for a new trial was denied and Stout's execution was scheduled for October. A public movement arose, to commute his sentence from death by hanging, to life imprisonment. Some of Rochester's most prominent citizens, including Susan B. Anthony and Frederick Douglass, petitioned New York Governor King on the matter. In October 1858, shortly before the execution, Anthony and Douglass invited the nationally known, anti-capital punishment supporter, Aaron Powell, to Rochester to speak in Corinthian Hall. He tried for three nights to speak, but each time, it ended in a public brawl. Unsuccessful efforts were made by Margaret Stout as well. She was released from jail in July 1858 and made a journey to Albany, to plead with the governor. She too was refused.

Stout was apparently determined not to accept the fate of the court. He at least twice tried to get help from visitors to the jail, wanting to take his own life. The first time, a woman smuggled poison into Stout's cell and then for some reason, took it herself. She survived. Another time, Stout slashed his wrists with a blade passed to him by a visitor. A guard saw his bleeding wrists just in time.

The Execution

On October 22, 1858, Ira Stout was hanged for the murder of Charles Littles.

Early in the day, Stout said his good byes to his family. In the early afternoon, Stout was led to the gallows. In the presence of one hundred spectators, most of them invited dignitaries, the rope was placed around his neck and a cap drawn over his face. The *Union and Advertiser* described it:

> *All being ready and the spectators standing in breathless silence, at twenty minutes past three o'clock Sheriff Babcock pulled the fatal line, and Ira Stout was suspended three feet from the floor. Not a sound was heard in any direction, save the heavy fall of the weight which did the fatal work. The death of the ill-fated man was not as sudden as could be desired though. His struggled for eight or ten minutes and caused the spectators to turn away in disgust. His neck was probably not dislocated, and he most probably died by slow strangulation.*

The following day, an odd story appeared in the newspaper.

> *A rumor was current last night at a late hour that Stout was not dead, and that efforts were being made to resuscitate him by the use of galvanic batteries and other means sometimes employed for the restoration of persons supposed to be dead. How much truth there is in the rumors thus made we cannot say, as we have not taken pains to inquire at the house of Mrs. Stout.*

Stout was laid to rest in an unmarked grave in Section D of Mount Hope Cemetery. Although she had fallen on hard times, Margaret Stout saw to it that her son had a proper burial. The cemetery plot reportedly cost five dollars, which Margaret paid, though she could not afford a grave marker. There are few markers in that section of the cemetery. Stout lies near another of Rochester's infamous killers, that of Octavius Barron, the murderer of William Lyman.

The High Falls Murder

Margaret Stout had a difficult time after her son's death. On June 1, 1859, The *Democrat and American* published "A Plea for Sympathy" on her behalf. It read:

> *The Democrat comes with an appeal to their readers' sympathies for Mrs. Margaret Stout who it appears is not permitted to labor where she is known or even to occupy apartments, and in consequence of the prejudice against her, she is on the verge of starvation. She has gone about from place to place in the city doing laundry work under an assumed name, and occupying such apartments as she could procure in the same way. She is shunned by everybody.*[25]

The outcome of this appeal is unknown. It is known that Sarah Littles was pardoned before her seven-year term at Sing-Sing ended. She subsequently remarried.[26]

Chapter 6

The Strange Defense
of Manley Locke

Honeoye Falls is a village within the town of Mendon in Monroe County, New York. Today its population is just under 3,000. The village, founded in 1791, includes a small waterfall on Honeoye Creek, which flows through the village and gives it its name. In October 1857, Benjamin Starr, a local constable was stabbed to death. His assailant was Manley Locke, a twenty-two year old man, whom Starr was attempting to arrest. The case "excited great interest," as one reporter put it, not only for the facts, but for Locke's somewhat novel defense.

The Trial

The trial began in October 1858. The facts of the case weren't much of an issue. The prosecution put on substantial witness testimony which elucidated the course of events. It was shown that Locke often carried a sharp knife with him, as well as a pair of "leaden knuckles." The murder was committed in the sight of witnesses. They testified that Locke had "high words" with Benjamin Starr Stark in Peach's Hotel, in Hot Falls, on the night of the murder. When Starr grabbed Locke to arrest him, Locke first struck Starr in the face with the "leaden knuckles," and then stabbed him. The coroner testified that the wound was located between the fourth and fifth ribs, and that Starr died within a few minutes. Others testified that Locke was intoxicated that night and that he attempted to escape, but he was pursued by bystanders and captured.

The real issues at trial concerned premeditation and what we would call today Locke's "mental state." In this sense, Locke was perhaps an unusual defendant. He was fully supported by his family, who testified that he had mental illness.

The *New York Times* covered the trial, noting:

> *The case derives particular interest because from the pressure of an array of family connections of the prisoner—a venerable grandfather from Michigan, uncles from Pennsylvania, Ohio, Kentucky, and Virginia, the young man's father, mother, sister and other relatives—all persons of very reputable standing, and all attentive spectators of the trial.*[27]

It was even more unusual that a "venerable" family tried to show that mental illness went back in the family, for generations. The defense argued that Locke was "never master of his actions; that at school he evinced no capacity for knowledge; that he has always been violent and headstrong: and that on one occasion, both his father and mother were in fear of their lives from him."[28] At trial, William G. Locke gave direct testimony on the younger Locke's long history of emotional difficulties and the first incident involving Locke and Starr.

> *He had spells of drinking; on these occasions when he thought we did not care anything about him he would carry that idea for two or three days; he was then dispirited and gloomy of following this directly he would most always commence to drink; when not in this state of mind he did*

not drink and did not pretend to go the village unless he had business there; previous to July 3, 1856, he had a spell of feeling bad and he would cry, saying that nobody cared for him and wanted him round; think he drank some at that time; on the 3rd of July he came to the house, I think between twelve and one o'clock., went to the drawer of table knives, took a knife out and went into the family room; I went up stairs for something, and when I came down he was talking with his mother and had his hand on her shoulder; he had a knife in his hand; and she said, "Manley, you would not hurt me, your mother?"

[I] think he made no reply; his eyes looked wild, and tears ran down his cheeks, he looked like a creature that was scared; when I came down he left his mother and came toward me, and said he must kill me; went out on the step, or platform, and he followed me out there, some ten or fifteen feet from the door and repeated that he must kill me; the tears ran down his cheeks; he went back into the house; I saw Mr. Valentine and asked him to see if he could get the knife away from him; Valentine went in and talked with him some; after a while he laid the knife up and sat down in a chair; his appearance when he followed me out was the same as when he was by his mother; he gave me no reason why he must kill me; he did not do anything when he said he must kill me; he had a knife in his hand, I kept my face toward him; after putting up the knife he leaned his head on a table in the dining-room, then went over to the depot and walked around on the platform; Mrs. Locke went downtown and saw Mr. Cummings, the magistrate; Mr. Starr, the constable, came and arrested him; he was taken in the depot; they took him to the village and then Starr brought him back, saying that fined him $10; I paid the fine and he was released; when Mr. Starr took the irons off Manley went over with me to the cars.[29]

The Strange Defense of Manley Locke

In 1857, the town of Honeoye Falls, New York, not only witnessed its first murder but also the first use of the novel defense of "inherited insanity".

One of the more important issues at trial was the issue of premeditation. It was claimed at trial that Locke had said, upon his release, if Starr "ever attempted to arrest [me] again, another star would shine." Thus one critical issue was whether the stabbing was the "fulfillment of a threat made."

Testimony was given by Locke's mother and an uncle, both of whom showed the young man had a long-standing "monomaniac tendency." In their view, the murder was not premeditated, but arose out of the events of that night. Some of the witnesses testified to indications of hereditary insanity in the Locke family going back three generations.

It is clear that it was a hard-fought trial, and Locke was well-represented. One reporter wrote:

> *Mr. Martindale commenced his summing up for the defence [sic] at the opening of Court yesterday morning, and spoke till 1 o'clock PM nearly five hours, when a recess was taken*

for dinner. At 2 o'clock in the afternoon, Court reassembled, and District Attorney Hudson spoke for the people until about 5 o'clock.

Judge Johnson's charge to the jury, occupied nearly an hour in delivery.

The impression seemed to prevail last evening that the case of insanity had been badly damaged by the rebutting evidence presented after the defence [sic] claimed their case and that the jury was largely in favor of conviction.

It was announced that the Court House bell would be rung, should the jury agree upon a verdict before 9 o'clock...The Jury did not come in, however, and at a quarter past nine the Court adjourned till this morning at half-past 8 o'clock...We learned that as the time of adjournment, the Jurors stood 10 to 2....[30]

It seems, however, that the reporter's sources, or his observations, were incorrect. When the jury came in, Locke was convicted, but not on the charge of murder. The jury found him guilty of manslaughter. Locke was remanded to jail to await sentencing.

Then the case took a brief unanticipated turn. On December 13, 1858, Locke escaped from jail, along with about fifteen other prisoners.

A newspaper reported the story under the headline "Manley Locke At Large Again."

The prisoners of this county had a general turn-out last night, and all who desired made their escape. Of the thirty-five prisoners in confinement, fifteen left—the rest declined to leave. The manner of escape was through a back window facing the river. They sawed of the iron bars in five places, and so made an opening about ten by sixteen inches through which they crawled, singly, and let themselves down ten or twelve feet to the water. The saws they used were made of watch springs, and two of them were found in the Jail this morning. How they obtained these implements we are not informed. They are small but very effective. The whole process for sawing was not done in one night. They had, doubtless, worked at it for several nights, and concealed the cutting by the use of tallow and coal dust, which would effectually hide the track of the saw. It is supposed that they fixed upon last night as the time for the stampede, knowing that Mr. Gatens, one of the night watch, had gone to the country to see his family, and so the force at the Jail was reduced.

We are told that Mr. Merrill, the Jailor, and two of his deputies went through the Jail at bedtime last night and supposed that all was right. They did not discover that an escape had been made until after daylight this morning. It is thought the rogues departed about midnight. If so, they had eight hours the start of the officers, who have gone into the country in all directions to seek for them.

The prisoners were mostly confined in separate cells, but the locks used upon the doors appear to be worthless. They were easily picked, and when one gained the hall he had no difficulty in liberating his companions. In some cases they picked the locks with a wire, in others they broke them with a stick of wood All the prisoners were invited to escape, but more than half declined to avail themselves of the proffer made. The rogues undertook to open the cell of Orren Whitney, under conviction for forging canal clearances, but he states that he forbid their doing so, and actually drove them away by threatening to give an alarm if they persisted in liberating him.

The escaping party wanted a rope with which to descend to the river, so they took the halter with which Ira Stout was executed. It has therefore served sixteen villains —fifteen more than was bargained for when it was procured by the Sheriff. The rope was saved, and may serve some of the party again. The water in the river back of the Jail is not three or four feet deep, and runs pretty swift. These fellows had to wade some twenty rods or more towards Court Street Bridge, before they could find a place to ascend the wall to dry land. They must have been

In 1824, Monroe County New York founded its first poorhouse to care for "the raving maniac, the young child and the infirm old man". Manley Locke was sent there to await his trial.

in a very uncomfortable predicament when they left the water. Those who have hamlets in the city no doubt repaired to them and changed their apparel before taking flight.

Later—This morning, says the Union of the 15th, Sheriff Babcock received a telegram from N. Dennison, of Mt. Morris, announcing that he had captured a person who he supposed was Manley Locke. A later dispatch states that citizens of Mr. Morris who had seen Locke, fully identified him. [31]

Finally, in early January 1859, Manley Locke learned his fate.

This morning, at half past nine o'clock, Manley Locke was brought into the Court of Oyer and Terminer to receive sentence under the conviction of manslaughter in the first degree, found at the last term of said Courts. The prisoner was attended by his sister, one of his uncles, and by J.H. Marsondale, Esq., his counsel.

The Strange Defense of Manley Locke

There was nothing extraordinary about the circumstances attending the killing. It was done with a common shoemaker's knife. The District Attorney had admitted that if the case was no murder, it was manslaughter in the third degree....[He] went on to say that Locke was a person of weak mind, and [though] judicially held answerable for murder, the court should take into consideration the condition of the prisoners, as shows by the evidence on the trial. He appealed to the court on behalf of the relatives of the prisoner, who were worthy of pity and would suffer most by the infliction of a severe sentence.

There was a consultation of half an hour among the members of the Court—a diversity of opinion, doubtless, existing among the four occupants of the bench as to the case. The Statutes were consulted, and at length the Court ordered the prisoner to be brought forward.

Locke stood up and was sworn that he was an American by birth, 22 years old, could read and write, no trade. Had religious instruction as an Episcopalian.

Judge Strong then said: Manley Locke, you have been indicted for murder—taking the life of Mr. Starr, an officer, while in the discharge of his duty; you were tried by a Petit Jury, and found guilty of manslaughter in the 1ˢᵗ degree. Have you anything to say why the sentence of the law should not be pronounced against you?

Locke: I have nothing to say.

The sentence of the Court is that you be sent to Auburn State prison for a sentence of life [32]

Thus Manley Locke put on what can only be called a successful defense of hereditary insanity. He then disappears, so far as can be determined at this writing, from the historical record.

Chapter 7

The Woman Who
Poisoned Her Family

The town of Batavia is the seat of Genesee County, with a population today of nearly 16,000. The name is derived from the Latin word for the Betuwe region of the Netherlands, and indicates the Dutch land developers who first moved there. It was the first town founded in the region and played a vital role in the early  nineteenth century, serving as the core of development as the region grew. It was the site of the notorious disappearance of Captain William Morgan in 1826, which gave rise to national political developments. A generation later, another case drew the attention of residents and authorities. In the summer of 1856, Polly Hoag (later, Polly Frisch) lost to mysterious illness not only her young daughter, but her husband as well. Over the next couple of years, the facts would emerge.

In 1844, Polly Franklin married Henry Hoag, in the town of Alabama in Genesee County. Over the decade from 1846 to 1856, she gave birth to eight children. Only two of her children would survive to adulthood. The cause of death for the first three children remains unknown to this day. And in the mid-nineteenth century, when death rates for children were high, the fact of such losses didn't necessarily point to any failure—or deliberate act—on the part of parents.

In the summer of 1856, Polly's husband, Henry, became ill and died in July. Shortly thereafter, Polly's six-year old daughter, Frances became ill as well. She died in August. Some neighbors and authorities were concerned, but there wasn't any proof that the deaths were deliberate. And there was also widespread belief that a woman wouldn't go so far as to murder her own daughter and husband.

In fall of 1856, Polly was remarried to a local man named Otto Frisch.[33] The following summer, for reasons that remain unknown, Henry's family came and took his two older children away. Nine-year-old Albert went to live with his an uncle, Lyman Hoag in Michigan. Seven-year-old Rosalie was sent to live with a family in Chautauqua County. The baby, Eliza Jane, was left with her mother and stepfather.

In October 1857, Otto became ill. When he realized he had the same symptoms that had afflicted his wife's family the summer before, he immediately sought medical advice. The doctor told him that he had been poisoned and gave him an antidote, which cured him. As soon as he was able, Otto left the country for Canada. There, he told people that his wife had tried to poison him.[34] Two-year-old Eliza Jane also became ill early that same month, and she died on October 20, 1857. Stanley E. Filkins, Henry Hoag's cousin, lived nearby. He contacted the Genesee County District Attorney's Office and relayed his concerns about Eliza Jane's death. An intensive investigation began immediately. Initially, the coroner's inquest was scheduled for October 22, 1857, but it was repeatedly delayed as new evidence continued to surface.

On November 9, 1857, Polly Frisch, then in her early thirties, was arrested by Genesee County Sheriff Alvin Pease. Thus began one of the longest, and strangest, series of court cases ever seen in western New York, or anywhere, for that matter.

Three days later, Frisch was brought to the Genesee County Court House in Batavia. For six days, Judge Augustus Cowdin listened to the evidence against her. The state put on the testimony of ten witnesses. The judge ruled there was sufficient evidence to hold Frisch, and she was remanded to the county jail. Frisch's father retained the legal team of Wakeman & Bryan, one of the best in the region, to defend his daughter. This legal team would see her through to the end.

Polly Hoag lived in the town of Alabama, located in Genesee County, New York. It was here that six of her children and husband would die. Neighbors always thought unusual events occurred in the house.

Legal Proceedings

The coroner's inquest would reconvene on January 19, 1858. Over the previous two months, the bodies had been exhumed and autopsied. Dr. Oliver P. Clark, a physician and pharmacist in Batavia, did chemical analyses on the contents of the stomach. After conducting three separate chemical tests, Clark found what everyone had suspected: arsenic. The grand jury was in session for two days. And in February 1858, Polly was indicted on three charges of first degree murder, in the deaths of her first husband, Henry Hoag, and her two daughters, Frances and Eliza Jane Hoag.

On June 30, 1858, after a series of delays, some of which were because Polly was ill, the trial for the murder of Henry Hoag began.[35] The courtroom was densely packed as Polly was brought in by the sheriff. The newspapers reported every detail, including that Frisch wore a black silk dress, black satin bonnet, a white shawl, and jet-black bracelets and necklace. She appeared calm.

Among the witnesses who would testify against her was her son.

The *Genesee County Herald & Spirit of the Times*, among others, printed detailed transcripts of the testimony. Though medical doctors described the effects of arsenic poisoning, there was conflicting testimony about whether Henry had displayed such symptoms. At issue, moreover, was whether Henry's symptoms might have been caused by an accident he'd had on the farm at about the same time, and which might have caused an internal injury. There was testimony supporting the prosecution's assertion that the marriage was unhappy, and that Polly might have been having an affair. But there were no eyewitnesses to the poisoning.

The jurors came back with a verdict of not guilty.

As the *Rochester Democrat* reported, "There appeared to be no doubt on the part of the spectators or the jury of the guilt of the prisoner, but the evidence did not warrant a conviction."

Polly was returned to jail, to await trial on the next murder charge.

In all, she would have five separate trials. The second trial was for the murder of Eliza Jane. She was acquitted, in a directed verdict from the bench. The third trial, for the murder of Frances, resulted in a hung jury. The fourth trail, again for the murder of Frances, resulted in a conviction. As one of Frisch's attorneys put it, "a re-exhumation of the deceased and a new analysis of the stomach...turned the scales."[36] But improper statements were made to the jury by the judge, and the verdict was overturned on appeal. Yet another trial was ordered.

Polly Hoag would later remarry. Her second husband would soon complain of a strange illness. Later she would be found guilty of multiple murders and sentenced to death.

At the fifth trial, the defense for the first time used a defense of insanity. Many years after the case, Frisch's attorney explained the reasoning.

She was indicted for the murder by arsenical poison, of Henry Hoag, her former husband, and her two children, Eliza Jane, aged about two years, and Frances, aged nine years. Her husband was about thirty-eight, and she thirty-three years of age. She always lived kindly with Hoag, and was apparently attached to these children. She had the bodies of her husband and children removed from the old graveyard to the new cemetery, paid for the new lot herself, bought tombstones, which she paid for in sewing, and left a little space between Hoag's and little Frankie's graves, where she was to be buried. She never attempted to escape, and always denied her guilt. When the accusations against her first became current, she called at our office and insisted upon having a slander suit brought against certain parties; and requested that the bodies be disinterred and analyzed.

From careful inquiry, we were satisfied that, on the evidence treating her as sane, she could not be convicted; for there seemed to be an utter want of sane motive for the commission of the triple murder. Being struck with her appearance, however, and before the first trial, I requested the late lamented and venerable physician, Dr. John Cotes, to examine her with reference to her mental soundness. He kindly did so, and reported that, although she was a very singular person, and of marked idiosyncrasies, he would not venture to advise us to rely at all upon insanity as a defense.

On this last (fifth) trail, Mr. Martindale was employed to assist Mr. Wakeman and myself. During the examination, some expressions of the accused, evincing increased happiness since the death of her husband and children, were proved, which, however, struck Mr. Martindale with force; for if true, as we were all inclined to think, there were strong indications that she was of a disordered mine.

The Woman Who Poisoned Her Family

We at once telegraphed to Dr. Cook, Superintendent of the Insane Asylum at Canandaigua, who came and examined the prisoner. Her family physician being then here from the West...Dr. Cook was able to ascertain her former habits and condition, and pronounced her insane. Drs. L.B. Cotes, Root, and Griswold, testified to the same effect, while others expressed great doubts as to her sanity. But, as I feared and anticipated, the very late period when this defense was set up, and the prejudice always existing against those cases not obvious to the plainest understanding, could not be overcome; and the jury, believing her sane, convicted the prisoner, and she was sentenced to die. Such, however, was the difficulty in find a motive for the crime that the jury hesitated for thirty-six hours before coming in with their verdict.[37]

Two years after she was first arrested, Frisch was found guilty of the murder of her daughter, Frances. She was sentenced to be hung on November 2, 1859. The jury, however, did not want to be responsible for the first hanging of a woman in the country. They petitioned the court and New York Governor Edwin D. Morgan for mercy. Governor Morgan responded to the petition by requesting that a certain Dr. Hall perform a mental evaluation of the prisoner. The report, which was widely reprinted in newspapers, read in part:

I have visited Polly Frisch, now confined for murder in the jail at Batavia...to ascertain whether she is of sound mind, and what was probably her mental condition during the commission of her crimes, and hereby respectfully report as follows...I visited Batavia three times...and personally examined her under different circumstances. I also went over the whole of the evidence bearing upon the subject of her insanity, and obtained new evidence which was important in helping me to decide so peculiar a case. In these examinations I received much assistance...in regard to the habits and conditions of the prisoner...From the information thus obtained (which only a personal examination of several weeks could have made clear) I am convinced that the prisoner, Polly Frisch, is now, and has for several years been subject to a form of insanity which is frequently the result of epileptic disease. This is now plainly apparent, and I think if attention had been called to this form of mental disease as a solution of her unnatural scheme, she would have been as much an object of sympathy and pity as of horror and aversion. I have thought it proper to send you the accompanying abstract of the prominent facts in the this peculiar case so that your Excellency may be able to form some judgment of the correctness of my conclusion. Edward Hall....[38]

Governor Morgan accepted Hall's conclusions and commuted Frisch's sentence to prison "for the term of her natural life."[39]

Frisch was then sent to Sing-Sing, where she remained until 1877, when she was transferred to the Kings County Penitentiary. In 1892, after many years there, Dr. Homer L. Bartlett, the attending physician at the penitentiary, petitioned the governor for Frisch's release, assuring him "that whatever might have been her mental condition at the time of the commission of the crime or afterward, she is now and for many years has been perfectly sane, and there is no reason to believe that she will ever become otherwise." It was further noted that she had:

...served an imprisonment of more than thirty-three years. During her imprisonment at the penitentiary she has been employed almost constantly in the hospital, where she has been of great service. She is now quite old and feeble...The District Attorney who prosecuted her recommended some years ago that she be released, and several persons of the highest respectability have undertaken to provide her with a suitable home.[40]

Governor Roswell P. Flower responded on December 9 of that year, and pardoned her. She was released. While several newspapers covered the story[41], with whom and where Frisch went remains a mystery.

Chapter 8

The Execution of Charles Eighmey

Oaks Corners, New York is exactly what it sounds like, a community grown up at the intersection of two roads. Today, there isn't much more than a post office and a few houses. It is not much changed from when Charles Eighmey moved there, a boy of six, onto a farm about a mile north of Oaks Corners[42] in the 1850s. Eighmey's parents ran the farm, and the young man worked on it as well as hiring himself out to neighbors to help on their farms. In 1874, Eighmey was working on the farm of George Crandall. An argument broke out and shortly thereafter, he was under arrest, charged with murder. The case was notable for its legal turns, including inconsistent testimony by witnesses who were arguably biased, and for accusations against another man, made by many. But the case is particularly remembered because Eighmey himself reiterated those accusations as he stood on the hanging scaffold.

The Crime

In the summer of 1874, a local newspaper reported:

> *Our community was startled last evening by the report that a bloody altercation had occurred between Charles Eighmey (pronounced Amey) and George Crandall, near Oaks Corners, and during the afternoon. The report proved but too true by later and more authentic accounts. It seems that Crandall, who owns a small farm near the corners, had Eighmey in his employ having hired him for the season. A wordy and acrimonious quarrel took place previously at the house, of which Mrs. Crandall was a witness, and she was so incensed at the conduct of Eighmey that she advised her husband to discharge him at once. But the latter declined, saying that he needed him, had engaged in for the season, and must keep him.*
>
> *They went to work together after dinner, hoeing potatoes. Subsequent reports of what occurred between them come only from one source, from Eighmey. He says that the quarrel was renewed and became more acrimonious than before, and that finally Crandall attacked him with a hoe. He says he warded off the blow in self-defense and struck back with the blade of the hoe which took effect upon his employer's head; that in the heat of passion he struck several other blows, he don't [sic] know how many, but probably all took affect [sic], when Crandall fell bleeding and insensible at his feet. He then went to the house and gave notice of the affray and that Crandall was badly injured.*
>
> *Neighbors were rallied and the insensible form of Crandall was taken to his house. Dr. Howe of Phelps was immediately summoned, who, upon examination, found that in two or three places the hoe had penetrated to the brain, while on the left side and on the back of the neck other blows had cut several of the smaller veins from which the victim had suffered a heavy loss of blood.*

The Execution of Charles Eighmey

Eighmey submitted to the immediate arrest. He is an unmarried man, aged about twenty-three years, and the youngest son of an honest hard-working farmer of the same neighborhood, Mr. Wiley Eighmey. Much doubt prevails as to the truth of Eighmey's statements, from the fact his person bears scarcely perceptible scratch.

But we will not prejudge the case, as it will in time undergo thorough investigation. Crandall, as already will have been conceived by the reader, is a married man — aged about forty-two years, oldest and only surviving son of our well known townsman Ambrose Crandall; everybody knows that the injured man was not naturally of a quarrelsome disposition, and it must have been most aggravated persecution that led him to assault if he really began it. His case is critical in the extreme. A report was in circulation early this morning that he died last night of his wounds, but subsequent accounts represent that he is still alive, and unconscious, and that there is but slight hopes of his recovery.[43]

Perhaps the most striking thing about this account is that Crandall was indeed widely known to be of a "quarrelsome disposition," which would soon be made clear in testimony.

Crandall died one day after he was beaten. A coroner's inquest was convened.

The coroner testified that there were "wounds inflicted on the head and neck of George L. Crandall...by an ordinary field hoe...Said wound penetrating the brain through different portions of the skull, causing... death."[44]

Mrs. Crandall gave a detailed account of events that day:

I was the first person there. Mr. Chas. Eighmey was working with him, hoeing potatoes, he was hired by Mr. Crandall to work on his farm. I think the injury was received about 2 o'clock. I went up stairs after dinner...I went into the bedroom, where there was a window facing the lot toward the west and happened to look out the window, I saw Chas.

Eighmey coming toward the house holding his hands together. I looked but did not see Mr. Crandall. I came down and went out the back door and called to Chas. Eighmey and asked him where is George?

...He stopped and I asked him where George was, and he answered me, that he was in the lot. I said where[?], I cannot see him. He then said, laying in the lot...I said you haven't hurt him have you...He commenced crying and said I am afraid I have...I went where George lay....

I found George Crandall's body laying with his head toward the east and feet to the west. There is not a path through the lot, I did not disturb the body when I got there, I took his head and laid it on my lap, I did not move him, I am sure he lay as stated....I saw a broken hoe laying by George Crandall. I did not notice his hat. I did not notice the ground. After Chas. Eighmey took his head, I went for Mr. B.F. Webster who was in his field south. I came back to where George lay, Mr. Webster came a little ahead there were several men there when I returned.[45]

As suggested by Mrs. Crandall's testimony, details would be an issue at trial, particularly the condition of the "lot," that is, the garden plot where the two men were working when the altercation ensued. These were at issue because Eighmey claimed he struck Crandall in self-defense. Disturbed ground would indicate a struggle, as Eighmey claimed there was. And whether Crandall's body was moved after he fell might show that Eighmey had attempted to "stage" the scene after the fact.

Questions having to do with the relationships between the parties were implicit in testimony at the coroner's inquest, and would continue through the trial. There were questions about the state of marriage, and particularly the role of a neighbor, Frank Webster. Eighmey had worked for Webster as well, beginning about three years before.[46]

Webster, who had seen Crandall and Eighmey working together in the potato field earlier in the day, also testified at the inquest.

The Execution of Charles Eighmey

The Charles Eighmey trial was held in Canandaigua, New York. The prosecution alleged a lovers triangle as the motive for the murder.

I was called by Mrs. Crandall about...one hour after I saw them...I went over to the potato field. There was no other person there except Charles Eighmey, except Mrs. Crandall who was with me. I found Mr. Eighmey holding Mr. Crandall's head upon his knee, and his head badly chopped up. He lay with his head to the south, straight out, legs close together, and hands by his side. His body lay on the row, and the head on Eighmey's knee, sitting on a hill of potatoes. I saw the broken hoe, it lay by the side of Mr. Crandall's leg—the hoe was broken and the piece lay beside to each other.

Mr. Eighmey and William Eighmey came there while I was there, there had been no change in position of body after I came[:] he was laying on his back, I saw marks of violence.

I saw gashes on forehead, 2 or 3 or more. I saw a gash on left side of face extending from upper portion of lower jaw downwards on side of neck....I assisted in carrying the body to the house. There was no apparent consciousness of Mr. Crandall...I asked Mr. Chas. Eighmey what he did this for.

He said that Crandall...struck him with the hoe and that he had to do it. I said to him you did not have to do it, why did you not run and leave him. He undertook to make further explanation and I told him to shut up....[47]

Webster's question to Eighmey, "Why did you not run and leave him?" points to the fact that there was a long history of difficulties between the he and Crandall. Eighmey had in fact "run away" from Crandall many times before, as would be made clear in further testimony. At the close of the inquest, Eighmey was indicted for the murder of George Crandall.

The Trial

Eighmey's trial began in May 1875. The *Geneva Courier* summarized the issues at hand:

After the jury was sworn, Dist. Attorney Hicks addressed them briefly, saying there was no living witness to the murder, that it was only upon circumstantial evidence and the testimony of the defendant that he could be convicted; that the people proposed to show that the crime was not committed in self-defense, that the trouble grew out of intimacy of the prisoner with the wife of Crandall, and that Eighmey had threatened to kill Crandall if he ever accused him of improper intimacy with her.[48]

Eighmey's threat suggests something of the relationship between them. Crandall apparently routinely and maliciously accused him of various things, including an interest in his wife. Eighmey vehemently denied this interest, and —as suggested by newspaper coverage— had sought the advice of others, including Mrs. Crandall herself and Webster, on how best to deal with Crandall. Crandall was thus clearly well-known to be a difficult person.

In fact, besides the relationships amongst those on the farm that day, many relationships —especially between the victim's family and those who investigated, prosecuted, and even defended the accused— were at issue throughout the case. For over two years, the case wound its way through the court system, a relatively long time in those days, when arrest, trial, and execution might follow a crime within a couple of months. As one student of the crime put it:

> *Eighmey was from the only family in that country neighborhood who were not related to the others. Charley admitted striking George twice in self-defense, but that did not explain the eleven ghastly gashes that penetrated George's head. Several conflicts of interests are apparent. The investigating officer was the cousin of the victim. [And] Charley's defense attorney was also found to be representing the estate of the deceased man.*[49]

In any case, testimony established that in the spring of 1873, Crandall proposed to Eighmey that the younger man take about three acres of land work to work on shares. Eighmey did so, and occasionally called on the Crandalls and likewise occasionally worked for Crandall. In the spring of 1874, Crandall proposed that Eighmey come and live with them and work the entire farm on shares. Eighmey moved onto the farm in April. Things went well for a couple of months, and then Crandall began to treat him badly. It was alleged that Webster, a neighbor, played a role in this, perhaps stirring up Crandall's suspicious nature.[50]

Testimony showed that Eighmey and Crandall had a difficult working relationship, squabbling over money and the division of chores. Crandall appeared to have been a very difficult man to work for. As one observer noted, "Evidence was introduced as to Crandall's character, which showed he was a boisterous and very profane man."[51] Defense witnesses testified that Crandall had threatened Eighmey. Others, including Eighmey's father, testified that he was a "quiet and peaceable young man." In riveting testimony at trial, Eighmey testified in his own defense. He painted a picture of a profane and threatening boss, and of himself as a man who knew he should walk away from the job permanently but couldn't. In the weeks before the fatal encounter, the relationship was clearly growing dangerous. Eighmey testified about the events of a day a couple of weeks before the murder.

> *[Crandall said]...You better get out of here entirely, you G–d d–d lazy pup, you want your d–d head knocked off from you, and I just as soon do it as to look at you; said he, get out of here, d–n you, don't come around me to-day; I said all right, and started down to the house, right across, and went to the house, and went hoeing in the garden....*

> *He picked up the iron rake and came down towards where I was and he said he, you don't know where that hoe is? No sir; I don't; think you had it around on south side of barn hoeing out the ditch...said he, G–d d–d you, do you tell me I left the hoe around there? No, I said, I don't tell you [that] you left it around there. Said I, I don't know, there is the last place I saw it, and perhaps it is there now.*

> *Well, said he, for just two cents I would sliver this garden rake right through you.*

> *Well, I said, I don't know anything about it; I don't know what I've done to you for you to have occasion to do anything of the kind; and, said I, I don't know how I am going to get along; I don't see any way but we'll have to settle up, I don't want to live in this way...*

> *I said, with jawing every day or two, and he raised the garden rake and made a dive for me, and I was standing beside the pear tree, and if I remember right he said G–d d–n you, I'll smash your brains out of you, very much in that way...I stepped behind this tree and said I, you're not going to hurt me, are you? I don't want you to hit me, I say. Said he, I'll show you whether I'll hit you or not....*

Eighmey's defense lawyer asked, "Up to that time had you really believed he would strike you?" Eighmey responded:

The Execution of Charles Eighmey

Yes, I had...I thought of it a great many times in my own mind, whether he would or he wouldn't; I couldn't get it through my head, of course, which way he meant, but he would use these expressions, and finally at least I began to get kind of afraid of him, and kept out of his way whenever I could; wherever I found work alone to do, I would always be doing it.[52]

The night before the fatal altercation, Crandall and Eighmey got into a dispute about Mrs. Crandall, who had left to visit her sister. When Crandall arrived at the house, he asked him about his wife's whereabouts.

Well, little Smarty hasn't got home yet [Crandall said.] I said, I don't know who you mean, George. He said, little Smarty...I said, I understood her to say she was coming home early tonight; said I, she will probably be home in a very few minutes for all I know.

Says he, G–d d–n her. Whenever she gets another horse of me to go away she will know it. Well, I said, I don't know anything about it, said I, I cannot tell anything about it when she will be home, nor when she went; it is none of my business....

I was going to the barn to help him unhitch; we drove them in the barn, and I was on the east side of the horses in the barn, and there was a three-tined pitch-fork on the west side and as I stepped up to unhook the tug, I said, I don't know anything about it, George...

Said he, G–d d–n you, you stick up for her. Said I, I haven't said anything. Said he, G–d d–n you get out of this barn or I will run the pitch-fork through you, and at that he gets it and comes right around and comes at me and says, I will run it through you. I said, I will get out, and I started out and stepped out pretty lively, and then I started and went up to the house, and he stepped to the door and said, if you ever come around me again in this barn, said he, I will take a pitch-fork, or anything I can get hold of and split your brains out and cut you from one end to the other.[53]

Nevertheless, the next day, found the two working together again in the potato field. According to Eighmey's testimony, Crandall complained again about his wife. According to Eighmey, he left to get water, in an attempt to defuse the situation. But when he came back, Crandall said:

> *I suppose you have been down to see little Smarty. You could not get along without going to see her.*

> *I said, I didn't not see her. I did not go the house to see her; I did not see her at all.*

> *Well, what in the hell did you go for?*

> *I said, I brought you up some water, and offered you the pail, and you did not notice it or anything...*

> *I hoed fast to keep ahead. At that time he kept telling me–I don't remember just what words he used, but I remember his saying, G–d d–n you, you won't be hanging around me a great while.*

> *...Then he gained within, perhaps 30 or 40 feet, and, said he, G–d d–n your soul, you want the brains knocked out of you, and I think I am the man that can do it...*

> *I turned, and instead of hoeing right the way I was hoeing, I turned around and faced him partly backwards in hoeing the potatoes and he then kept gaining right onto me...*

> *He said, I shall split your G–d d–n brains open and struck me a second time; and I warded off the blow the first time— partly knocked me down and gathered up and brought my left hand and hoe together in some shape and warded his blow off with it, and his hoe then cut my hand and cut it right between the thumb and forefinger; you can see the scar there now; then I struck him and knocked him down, and he partly gathered on his hands and feet in some shape and said he—let me see, kind of gathered up—said he, I will split the brains right out of you; I will kill you I will kill you, law or no law....*

The Execution of Charles Eighmey

Charles Eighmeys execution was the first in Ontario County's history. The rope used in Eighmeys hanging had been used five previous times including the execution of Ira Stout.

Then I don't remember...I didn't know anything about it, how many times; I had no more idea of it, no way, shape or manner, of striking him; I only knew I struck him twice. I never remembered anything about my striking him any after that; I didn't know as I done it.[54].

Eighmey's claims of self-defense did not persuade the jury. He was convicted and sentenced to be executed on July 2, 1876. His lawyers, J.P. Faurot and John Bean, obtained a stay of execution and made motion for a new trial. In April 1876, the motion was denied. In May, Eighmey was again sentenced to death. Faurot then sought a stay and commutation from the governor of New York, Samuel J. Tilden. The stay was initially granted, but the commutation was not.[55] The execution was scheduled for August 11, 1876.[56]

The Execution

Newspapers covered the last day of Eighmey's life in detail.

Wednesday had been a trying day for Eighmey. He had parted for the last time with his father and had received many callers, and had his fortitude severely tried. Yet he ate heartily, and afterward smoked a cigar with apparent relish. He engaged in conversation with one of his attendants, Mr.

Tate. He talked freely about the final disposition of his body; said that he desired to be buried in Phelps by the side of his sister. He was very solicitous about the expense of the funeral, and said he hoped his father would be saved that expense, as he had already been the cause of reducing him to poverty. About midnight he retired and slept calmly and quietly until six o'clock.

From early in the morning until sundown, crowds of people passed and re-passed the jail, scanning the high walls of the jail yard to see if they could not discover some trace of the preparations for the tragedy of the morrow. There were many applications to Sheriff Boswell for admittance to the yard to see the gallows, but with the exception of some of the foreign representatives of the press, they were uniformly refused. No one was permitted to see Eighmey, except his relatives, spiritual advisers, and those he requested to see.

Rev. Mr. Green, of Geneva, formerly pastor of the Methodist Episcopal church of this place, was with him the greater part of the day. To him Eighmey expressed the utmost confidence in the future, he said he had a firm hope that he had found peace and salvation through his Savior; that he had no dread of death, but looked forward to it as a relief from the present. To our reporter he said, 'I shall be much happier tomorrow night than I am now.'

It must have been extremely trying, aside from the consciousness that it was the last he would pass on earth. In the morning his eldest sister Mrs. Parker, his brother, and brother-in-law called to take their final parting. The interview was inexpressibly touching and sad. Eighmey was by far the most collected; he told them not to mourn, that he was ready, that death had no terrors for him, and that he hoped to meet them in that bright land where there was no parting, or shadow of sorrow.

The Execution of Charles Eighmey

Among his last acts Eighmey wrote a note expressing his gratitude to the Sheriff, the members of the Sheriff's family, and the various attendants during his confinement, for their kindness to him.

His counsel, Mr. Faurot, during the long day, had his final interview with him. Although he had visited him daily, since the decision of the Governor, the parting was painful to both....

He ate heartily of his supper, and conversed cheerfully with his attendants upon various topics. He expressed a wish to Deputy Sheriff Frank Boswell, who was present, that the shackles might be removed from his limbs. This was cheerfully accorded, and he in company with our reporter, at once proceeded to Mr. Martin's, who returned with them, and removed the shackles. To do this it was necessary to cut the rivets that held them. There were four, and Eighmey presented one to each of his attendants, C. H. Tate and George McClary, and to Frank Boswell and our reporter. As soon as the heavy shackles (they weighed twelve pounds) were removed, he sprang up and walked rapidly across the room remarking, 'How light I feel.' Shortly after, he took a bath, and about eleven o'clock he retired. [57]

The morning of the execution "dawned dark and lowering, as if nature lamented the deed so soon to be enacted."[58] Eighmey's family arrived, and his two brothers requested to see him. But Eighmey "refused the request, fearing it would unman him."[59]

Another newspaper described the scene in detail.

The scaffold is on the west side of the jail yard, next to the wall. It is on a platform forty-two feet by eighteen in width, raised three feet from the ground surrounded by a railing, and is built on substantially the same plan as that used for the execution of John Clark lately in Rochester, though far superior to it in looks and construction. Through the cross-beam runs a rope, at one end the fatal noose, at the other end a weight of 225 pounds. This rests upon a trap that can be sprung with a wonderful ease, the whole being concealed behind a partition about five feet wide and twenty feet high. Here stands the person who launches Eighmey into eternity.

The rope has already a history of its own. It has been used at five hangings before. It has judicially strangled Ira Stout, Joseph Messner and John Clark, at Rochester, Rulloff, at Binghampton, and only three weeks ago to-day was used at the execution of Thomas B. Quackenbush, at Batavia....

By eight o'clock a crowd had assembled in front of the jail, and eager efforts were made to gain admission to the jail. Among these was B. F. Webster, who was clamorous in his demands for admission. The 8:45 train from Rochester, brought Company D., 54th Regiment, N. Y. S. N. G., Captain Moore commanding, and numbering 57 men, officers included. They marched directly to the jail, and were there stationed, guarding the street, and keeping back the throng. By half-past nine Jail [S]treet was a mass of pushing, crowded humanity, contrasting strangely with the bright uniforms of the soldiers. The roofs of the adjoining houses were covered with people, but fortunately their curiosity was defeated by the gallows being covered with canvas. The crowd, though orderly, did not seem very deeply impressed with the gravity of the occasion, for they laughed and joked as they pushed backwards and forwards.

The newspapers had, in the interim between verdict and execution, continued to pursue questions about the relationships of all those involved. It seems that both Mrs. Crandall and Webster had encouraged Eighmey to "stand up" to Crandall, and perhaps not to leave his employ. Given Crandall's character, this was clearly questionable advice, and raises the question whether one or both of them might have hoped for the outcome that arrived. Observers noted that Webster had visited Eighmey in jail at least three times before his indictment, and pledged each time to support the plea of self-defense. At trial, however, he did not do so.

The Execution of Charles Eighmey

At any rate, events on the scaffold that day—indeed, the manner in which Eighmey was portrayed in his last days—shows the sympathy with which Eighmey's contentions about Webster's complicity were met.

Last night to our reporter [Eighmey] said, when asked concerning Webster's and Mrs. Crandall's complicity in the crime, 'God knows it is true; do you think I would go to my death with a lie in my mouth?'

His entire conduct until he was summoned to the gallows was collected....At twenty minutes after ten B.F. Webster entered the jail yard; he showed no emotion, but conversed freely, he spoke about as follows in answer to questions by our reporter, and the reporter of the Rochester Democrat and Chronicle:

'Eighmey has lied from beginning to end, and he knows it. If he persists in it today I don't care a damn. He can't hurt me.' He claimed that the confession was inconsistent. He was very violent and profane, and evinced the utmost vindictiveness against Eighmey and left, by his manner and mode of speech, but a poor impression on his listeners.

Mortal man will never know whether he be innocent or guilty. But public opinion will be against him, and guilty or not guilty, the dying statement of Charles Eighmey will follow him as an avenging Nemesis through all his life.

At precisely twelve minutes of eleven the procession...filed into the yard and ascended the scaffold...Eighmey was dressed in full suit of black broadcloth, furnished by the Sheriff, and carried in his hand a beautiful bouquet, the gift of Mrs. Judge Taylor, on which was a card bearing the inscription 'The blood of Jesus cleanseth us from all sin.'

He was self-possessed and cool as any spectator. Not a muscle quivered, nor was his face blanched with fear; not a limb trembled as he ascended the scaffold. He cast one quick glance upwards at the awful implement of death before him. He passed along the platform and was seated in a chair beneath the fatal noose. The Sheriff Boswell then read the death warrant, and the subsequent stays of proceedings and final order from the Governor. During the time, Eighmey sat perfectly unconcerned.

The Sheriff then said, 'Charlie, have you anything to say?'

'I have,' he said.

Arising from the chair, he turned to under Sheriff Benham and whispered. Sheriff Benham stepped forward and called, 'Is Frank Webster here...and will he come forward.'

Webster stepped upon the scaffold, and stood facing the doomed man.

Then occurred the most dramatic scene ever witnessed at an execution. There stood the two men, both in the full flush of health and manhood, one under the gallows, on the verge of eternity — the other in the natural course of events with many years before him, and he, paler than his accuser. In a low, and perfectly clear voice, Eighmey said, all the time pointing his finger at Webster, 'The people of Ontario [C]ounty may have the privilege of thanking you for bringing me here to where I now stand, for you know what you told me, and you know that confession to be the truth, and you can't deny it. And now what is to be done with me? That what you and Mrs. Crandall talked to me, and got me into this trouble, which was against my will, and always was, as I told you. And now for me to take the penalty of this law and you go free; that it shall be — Well, I have nothing to say with reference to what shall be done with you, or anything of that kind, only as I say this — that what you did do, and talked to me, and as I made that confession, that each and every word of it is the truth, and nothing but the truth, and you know you cannot deny it, Mr. Webster. If Mrs. Crandall was here, she must always think of it — what she talked and told me.'

The Execution of Charles Eighmey

Eighmey stood holding the bouquet in his left hand, and so great was the control over his nerves, that his hand never even quivered. At the conclusion of the prayer, deputy-Sheriff Sheldon strapped his arms and legs. He submitted to it without a tremor. After it was finished he presented Mr. Green with his bouquet; then turning to Deputy-Sheriff Reed, whispered 'You know, Mr. Reed, Webster has brought this upon me.' Reed said, 'If you want to say anything, do so.'

Then with the noose dangling over his head, and his arms and limbs strapped, Eighmey spoke, in the same quiet collected manner and said, 'This crime I stand charged under was never done by my will, but under the influence of Charlotte Crandall and you, Webster, and you know it. The guards that have been in the jail and taken care of me have been all kind; and the sheriff and his family have treated me with kindness and respect, and the guards have all, too. I hope the people will always give them credit for being good to me. And my folks — my relations — have done all for me that lay in their power to do; and I hope we will all meet again, each and every one of us; and I hope I am forgiven of my trouble, and I think I am. I think I am going all easy and free.' (Here the prisoner's voice failed him.) After a moment he added: 'I bid you all goodbye.'

When he had finished, he turned and said to Under-Sheriff Benham, 'I am ready.' Mr. Benham then placed the noose around his neck, and pulled the black cap over his face, and at precisely 11:07 o'clock the signal was given and Charles Eighmey was launched into eternity.

His death must have been painless, as save a slight muscular contraction after the trap was sprung, there was no evidence of pain or the slightest struggle. After hanging 15 minutes, Drs. Simmons and Smith, attending physicians, pronounced him dead. Before the body was cut down, Sheriff Boswell announced that it was the request of Eighmey that his body should not be buried by the public, and asked those present to retire. The body was placed in a black walnut coffin, with silver plated handles, plainly mounted, and with a large silver plate bearing the simple inscription, Charles Eighmey, aged 26.

Much was made of Eighmey's statement to Webster, and it seems that he had not-inconsiderable sympathy.

The *Geneva Courier* noted in its follow-up story:

That which has attracted most of public attention, and will serve to keep alive the memory of this horrible affair, is the wonderfully dramatic scene at the gallows, in which the doomed man called forth Benjamin F. Webster, and charged the responsibility of the crime on him...

We have little disposition to pursue this subject. It is true that Eighmey perjured himself upon his trial. There are few who would not tell what they deemed the best story under like circumstances; and thus was destroyed in a measure Eighmey's testimony as against others. In any event there is scarce a palliating circumstance in his case, and he merited the punishment he received. On the other hand, we are not inclined at this time to review the present or past personal character of Mr. Webster — which it must be confessed has some very ugly spots — nor the extent to which his word will be received for truth by intelligent people where he is known, but would simply say that the opinion expressed below is the predominant one in the community....[60]

Charles Eighmey's funeral was held at the family residence the following Saturday. It was, a newspaper said, "largely attended, and the occasion was a very impressive one."[61]

Chapter 9
The Woman Who Got Away With Murder

A nineteenth-century gazetteer describes the town of Avon, New York, as celebrated for its mineral springs and having three churches, five large hotels, and 879 inhabitants.[62] First settled in 1785, today it is a bit bigger, with a population of over 4,000, and with twice as many churches. In 1877, L. Bradford Withey and his wife Rosetta were living near Avon with their four children. The elder Withey was a laborer, an alcoholic, and without income, except for a pension of $10 per month, given to him for injuries sustained during his service in the Civil War. His death was, in effect, the result of two separate crimes committed against him.

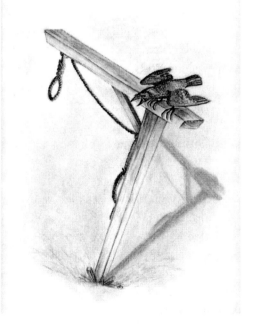

The Crimes

The first crime committed against Withey was when he was shot by his drunken teenaged son. A newspaper account describes the benighted Withey's circumstances:

> *In January, 1877, a son, 17 years old, of Mr. Withey, returned home from Avon somewhat under the influence of liquor. Withey attempted to exercise his authority over the boy, and the latter seized a shotgun and fired at his father. The charge entered Withey's face. Withey had been a soldier in the civil war, and had lost the sight of one eye from a wound received in the services. His son's shot put out the other eye, and inflicted other serious wounds. The boy was arrested, tried, and sentenced to three years in the penitentiary.*[63]

Withey was laid up, now totally blind and recovering from other injuries, when a neighbor, William Pierson, apparently stepped in to help. Pierson lived nearby, with his wife and four children. Thus the stage was set for the ultimate crime against Withey.

During the next month, Pierson spent "about half of his time" at the house, and he and Rosetta Withey, the sick man's wife, were together a great deal. According to witnesses, they held many whispered conversations and administered medicines to the sick man. For a time, Withey was improving. As a newspaper later reported, "He was so far recovered as to be able to leave his bed." On Saturday, January 27, Pierson took Mr. and Mrs. Withey to the village of Avon. Withey was left at the store of Smith & Hall, while Pierson and Rosetta went elsewhere. That day, it would later be revealed, Pierson purchased half-an-ounce of arsenic at Dr. William Nesbit's store. Pierson told the man that he wanted to kill rats.

The Witheys and Pierson returned to the house together later that day. That night Withey was taken violently ill. Over the following days, he was seen by a number of physicians, each of whom prescribed medicine. More than once, Withey appeared to be improving, but would only relapse. On one occasion, Pierson was overheard to exclaim, "By God, I wonder how much more he is going to bleed; he's bleeding like a stuck hog."

The Woman Who Got Away With Murder

On February 8, 1877, Withey died.

There was rumor swirling about the manner of his death, but nevertheless no investigation was done. Withey was buried without incident.

The Flight

On February 20, just eight days after her husband's death, Mrs. Withey abandoned her children and went to Rochester. She was joined there by Pierson, who had sold his property and abandoned his wife and children. Six days later, the two went to Jackson, Michigan, where they were married.

And with their disappearance from Avon, rumors increased. An investigation was begun. Withey's body was disinterred and an autopsy was done.

In October, both Pierson and Mrs. Withey were arrested and taken back to Geneseo, New York. They were both charged with murder, and more specifically, it was claimed that both he and Mrs. Withey, the wife of the murdered man, beginning on January 27, 1877, and on other days between that time and February 8, administered arsenic to Mr. Withey, with intention of causing his death.

They would be given separate trials.[64]

The Trials

The cases drew intense newspaper coverage because of the salacious details of an extra-marital affair, but also because of the legal twists and turns they took.

In February 1878, Pierson was put on trial, which lasted a week. One of the primary issues at trial was the nature of his relationship with Mrs. Withey. They had apparently been having an affair for some time, and it was "common rumor about the neighborhood that a criminal intimacy existed."[65]

He was found guilty and sentenced to hang in April.

Pierson's lawyers immediately appealed the conviction, so the execution was stayed.

Mrs. Withey went on trial in July 1878. There was considerable sympathy for her because she had four children. After a week of testimony, the jury acquitted her. They seemed to believe that Pierson alone gave the poison to her husband, wishing to seduce her. Mrs. Withey moved to Livonia, where she remained for many years.

In April 1879, Pierson's case reached the appellate level. His lawyers had appealed on the basis of testimony given by doctors. Thus, the case is known today partly because it marks a moment in case law, forcing a ruling on the then fairly new doctrine of doctor–patient privilege.

In his appellate ruling, which stayed the opinion of the lower court, Justice Earl described the facts this way:

> *While Withey was sick, suffering from the poison which is supposed to have been administered to him, Dr. Coe, a practicing physician was called to see him by the prisoner, and he examined him [Withey] and prescribed for him. On the trial, he [Coe] was called as a witness for the People, and this question was put to him: 'State the condition in which you found him at that time, both from your own observations and from what he told you?'*

> *The prisoner's counsel objected to this question on the ground that the information which the witness obtained was obtained as a physician, and that he had no right to disclose it; the evidence offered was prohibited by the statute.*

> *The court overruled the objection, and the witness answered, stating the symptoms and condition of Withey as he found them from an examination then openly made in the presence of Withey's wife and the prisoner, and as he also learned them from Withey, his wife and the prisoner. There was nothing of a confidential nature in anything he learned or that was disclosed to him.*

> *The symptoms and condition were such as might be expected to be present in a case of arsenical poisoning. It is now claimed that the court erred in allowing this evidence....It [the statute] could not have been designed to shut out such evidence as was here received, and thus to protect the murderer rather than to shield the memory of his victim.*[66]

Consequently, a new trial was denied to William Pierson. The judges of the county were directed to fix another day for Pierson's hanging, and the date was set for March 20, 1880.

Once again, Pierson's lawyer sprang into action, launching a commutation campaign. The *Mt. Morris Enterprise* summed it up this way:

> *Since his last sentence, Gen. Wood has labored untiringly to get the sentence of Pierson's commuted, and petitions were freely circulated in the county, and signed by about 2,400 people. Last week Thursday these petitions were presented to Gov. Cornell, and the General made a plea in Pierson's behalf for a commutation of his sentence....*

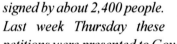

William Pierson had gone to buy a half an ounce of arsenic at Dr. Nesbit's office. He said he wanted to kill rats.

> *Mr. Wood's argument in brief was: 1st, Pierson was convicted upon circumstantial evidence alone, and not of such a conclusive character as to render it certain that he was guilty; 2nd, That Mrs. Withey, who was jointly indicted with Pierson for the murder of her husband, was afterward tried upon substantially the same testimony, and was acquitted by the jury; 3rd, that under these circumstances the interest of both justice and of humanity forbade that Pierson's life should be taken but would be better sub served by a commutation of his sentence to imprisonment for life [because of]...the testimony of Laura Pierson, the wife of the condemned man, given upon the trial of Mrs. Withey, as to her sending arsenic instead of quinine by mistake, to be administered to the deceased during his sickness,*

*and also...as an explanation of the quantity of arsenic found in
the body of the deceased.*

*In opposition District Attorney Strang argued that the prisoner
had been fairly and impartially tried and convicted...The
evidence conclusively demonstrated the fact that Withey died
from the effects of arsenical poisoning, and that whatever might
be said as to the desirability of a quantitative analysis in such
a case, it did appear satisfactorily by the testimony of Prof.
Lattimore, that in the small parts of the viscera of the deceased
submitted to him for analysis, he found sufficient arsenic to
have caused Withey's death. That Pierson bought arsenic just
before Withey was taken sick, had an opportunity and motive to
administer it to him, and failed to account satisfactorily for the
arsenic so purchased by him in any other way. That the acquittal
of Mrs. Withey should have no bearing upon the case, inasmuch
as there was no positive proof upon her trial that she had any
arsenic in her possession, or that she had any actual knowledge
of its being administered to her husband, and this difference in
the proof warranted, if it did not justify, her acquittal.* [67]

The governor denied the request for commutation.

The Execution

The *Mt. Morris Enterprise* carried a lengthy account of the execution.
There were approximately fifty witnesses, with another four to five hundred
spectators milling in the courtyard. They described Pierson this way:

*He...awoke and asked what time it was and was told that it
was morning. He remarked 'that it was the last time he would
ever see the break of day.' He then called for Dan McCloud,
and in his presence broke down and cried like a child. The
night previous to his execution he ate a good hearty supper
probably too much, Friday for breakfast was the only able to
sip a little coffee, his stomach for the first time refusing food.*

At eight o'clock, when he was being shaved, he was taken sick and vomited, and was subject to attacks of vomiting for an hour or two afterwards. All morning and until his execution, Rev. Mr. Cale, of Geneseo, was with Pierson and labored with him in preparing him to meet his God....

At 12:35 the Sheriff's train marched quietly through the halls of the jail and stepped into the enclosures. Rev. Mr. Cole, of Geneseo, clad in a black robe led the way, followed by Pierson and Sheriff Linsley who had the prisoner by the arm. Pierson walked with a firm step to the platform under the gallows. He was cleanly shaved, worse a black suit and slippers, and in physique was a fine type of a perfect man. As he stepped upon the platform he put his hands to his eyes for a moment as if there was a blur before them. He stood facing the jury and apparently calm and unmoved. S.N. Heriges, Esq, of Dansville...then read the death warrant, and the prisoner listened composedly, no change of his features being discernible.

When asked what he had to say, he responded in a voice free from emotion or tremor: 'I have got nothing more to say than I am convicted wrongfully, and will be executed

Avon, New York was settled in 1785. In the center of the village stands a Civil War soldier standing atop a tall, tapered column. On the broader section near the base is written, "Rest here for the night".

for a crime I am not guilty of.' Rev. Mr. Cole then offered a prayer, with the prisoner kneeling, his head bowed in a chair. After the prayer he arose and stood erect without any assistance, and Sherriff Linsley first strapped his legs then pinioned is arms behind him, during which time he never moved a muscle or flinched, but placed his hand over his eyes for a moment, once or twice. Under Sheriff T. O'Meara then adjusted the noose to his neck, with the knot under the left ear, then placed the black cap over his head. During that time he took Sheriff Linsley by the hand and whispered to him several times.

Everything was now in readiness, the blocks were removed that held the plank, and the Sheriff walked about half the length of the plank when the trap sprung and the weight struck the ground with a dull thud, and the body of Pierson shot into the air, raising him about three feet above the platform. There was just a slight struggle for a few seconds, the muscles of his arms contracted and drew up a little, then assumed their natural position; his legs drew up a trifle and then straightened, then his body swayed a little and soon became almost motionless. Drs. Patterson, of Livonia, and W. Lauderdale, of Geneseo, took hold of each wrist: his pulse at three minutes was 120; at four minutes a slight tremor was felt, and at four and one-half, no pulse; at fine minutes there was a slight flutter, and not again was it noticeable until nine minutes, and then they pronounced life extinct, and his neck was broken, as an after-examination proved.

The body hung suspended twenty-two minutes, was then taken down and placed in the coffin. The plate on the coffin read: 'William B. Pierson, aged 35 years and 4 months.' W.C. Drake was to take charge of the body, and it was placed in the hearse of Mr. Wright, the undertaker at Avon, and conveyed to that place. [68]

Another newspaper captured the "lesson" of the case this way:

> *If there is a special moral to be drawn from this case, it is the awful warning which it suggests against he illicit relations which places men and women outside of pale of respectable society. Wm. Pierson's crime was prompted by his relations with Mrs. Withey and in order to remove all obstacles from their path, took the life of Withey.*
>
> *The tragedy...is a sermon against the unchastity which defiles the human characters, and prepares it for deeper crime. The lesson is plain and needs no analysis. In the fate of the murdered, across whose path now falls the shadow of the gibbet, there should be a warming against the first error which led the unfortunate man and woman to the path of doom.[69]*

Despite the overwhelming evidence of the guilt of both, only Pierson paid for the crime, and he declared his innocence from his arrest to his last moments on the scaffold.

Chapter 10

The Train Station Murder

The town of Macedon, not far from Palmyra, New York has today an area just over 23,000 acres with a gently rolling, irregular surface and a population of nearly 8,700. The town was founded in 1789. The Erie Canal played an important role in its settlement and growth, as it had two ports on the canal. The building and operation of the Erie Canal drew immigrants to all of western New York. The enormous difficulties faced by immigrants are painted clearly in the story of Anna Dickhof and her daughter Lizzie.

The murder was covered by the *New York Times,* which headlined the story, "Tragedy in a Railroad Station: A German Woman Kills Her Child and Seriously Wounds Herself."

The little town of Macedon, 18 miles from Rochester on the direct road east, is the scene of a tragedy most mysterious in its nature. Ordinarily that village is a very quite place, with

The Train Station Murder

Macedon, New York, was founded in 1789. The Macedon Grange is pictured here. Anna Dickhof was on her way to Macedon by train from Rochester to reunite with her husband.

scarcely anything to cause a ripple of excitement. A young German woman named Anna Dickhof arrived in the village yesterday afternoon on an emigrant train. She could not speak a word of English, and sat in the station house all night. No one disturbed her, and she was given a couch sleep upon with her little child, a girl 11 months old. This morning, about 4 o'clock, Baggage Agent Patrick Quinn heard a sound as if a woman was vomiting, and turning up the light in the waiting room, discovered the little child lying dead on the couch, with its throat cut from ear to ear, and a pool of blood upon the floor.

The mother also lay apparently lifeless, with arms extended and blood trickling down from a stab in her throat and staining her dress. On the floor near by was an open penknife, the blade of which was covered with blood. Leaving the mother and child untouched, Quinn ran to the village for a physician, and found Dr. Lacey, who at once repaired to the Central Station House at Macedon. Meanwhile Christian Dumtee, a constable of the village, was walking along the road leading from the village to the station house. About 200 rods south of the station he found a woman lying in the snow by the roadside insensible and covered with blood.

Returning to consciousness while Quinn was absent, the German woman had walked out of the station and had fallen where the constable found her. Mr. Dumtee at once removed her to the house of Richard Deyo, only a few rods distant, where she was when Dr. Lacey visited her. The child was dead, probably having lived but a moment after its throat was cut. The mother's would was found to be not so serious, as the knife had only been stabbed into her throat, inflicting a wound the size of the blade. The windpipe is partially severed, but the woman stands a fair chance of recovery.

The only explanation of the tragedy is that the mother murdered her child and then made an attempt at suicide. The infant was removed to Brundage's undertaking rooms, where an inquest will be held at 10 o'clock tomorrow morning. The motive for the crime is not apparent. In April…August Dickhof left his wife and a 2-months-old child in Berlin, while he came to this country and engaged as a farm laborer in the village of Lincoln. On the 13th of November he sent his wife, Anna, $27 to come with her child to this country. Lincoln is 10 miles from Macedon, and as August did not expect her so soon she found no one waiting for her when she arrived, and having no place to go, was compelled to remain in the station over night. Whether or not her act was the result of despondency in the belief that her husband had deserted her is only conjecture.

August Dickhof was informed of the tragedy and at once came to the village, only to find his child dead and his wife in a critical condition. When he was taken into the room where she

Apparently a simple mix-up in the date of her arrival accounted for Anna Dickof's husband not meeting her at the train station. This would result in a terrible tragedy.

lay she recognized him, and after an embrace said, in tones of agony, "Where is my little Lizzie? Bring me my little girl." All through the day she repeated the request, and toward evening became delirious and constantly called for her child. She is a remarkably handsome German woman, 24 years of age, and was neatly dressed. Her husband is two years her senior, and although he has been several months in this country, he is unable to speak English. He is heartbroken over this occurrence. It is believed that the woman did the horrible deed while temporarily insane.[70]

Unfortunately, we do not know what happened to the young mother afterward. Anna Dickhof disappeared from the public record, never to be heard from again.

Chapter 11

The Execution of Joseph Tice

In 1891, Joseph Tice, also known as "Daredevil Joe," lived in Rochester, New York, where he'd moved shortly after the Civil War. The city was entering a new era: the population was now over 130,000, and horse trolleys were giving way to electric cars. Kodak had started production of film, and Rochester Gas & Electric had started construction of electric subways.[71] The new technologies would factor into Tice's life in a way that he probably couldn't have imagined.

Born in Michigan in 1829, Tice had served honorably in the Fifth Michigan Calvary. In 1879, he had married Agnes Leggett in Rochester. Their marriage was tumultuous, with his wife leaving him repeatedly because of his drinking. In the summer of 1891, she'd left him yet again, while he was in jail, and taken a job as a domestic at a boardinghouse.

Tice had been arrested for public drunkenness, and after serving a month's sentence, he was released. He announced his intention to kill his wife if she refused to live with him again. He had, in fact, previously stabbed her and done

The Execution of Joseph Tice

The Monroe County Jail where Joseph Tice was housed waiting trial for murder. He would be eventually transferred to Auburn Prison and executed.

a term in the penitentiary for it. On that afternoon, Tice sharpened his knife and appeared at the boarding house where his wife worked. She evidently refused his entreaties, because he stabbed her three times. She died about thirty minutes later. Tice was soon convicted of murder and sentenced to death.

Today, the case is notable less for the facts of the case than Tice's own manner of death. He was sixty-three years old at the time of his execution, by a method that was then brand-new: electrocution. Tice was one of the first to die in the electric chair.

Tice was sentenced to die at Auburn Prison in early January 1892, and arrived there a few weeks before. He was granted a stay when his lawyers filed an appeal. Soon, the appeal was denied and execution was set for May 1892. Tice would be only the second man put to death in the electric chair. The state of New York had begun searching for an alternative to hanging about five years before and some employees of Thomas Edison had come up with an electric chair.

MURDER, MAYHEM, AND MADNESS

On August 6, 1890, William Francis Kemmler was the first man to be put to death in this way. Kemmler was raised in Philadelphia, the child of German immigrants, both alcoholics. The young man dropped out of school at age ten, was shortly thereafter orphaned, and remained illiterate his whole life. He became a heavy drinker and was well-known in Buffalo for legendary drinking binges. On March 29, 1889, Kemmler murdered Tillie Ziegler, his common-law wife, by beating her with a hatchet. He was tried, convicted, and sentenced to death by electrocution at New York's Auburn Prison. His lawyers had appealed the sentence, arguing that electrocution was cruel and unusual punishment. The legal argument caused a media sensation, not least because it drew official positions from George Westinghouse (a backer of alternating current) and Thomas Edison (a backer of direct current.)

And the issue of "cruel and unusual punishment" arose again after Kemmler's execution, for good reason. The execution had been, by all accounts, ghastly.

The *New York Herald* covered the story in detail, in an article entitled, "The First Execution by Electrocution in Electric Chair: Kemmler's Death by Torture; Twice the Current Was Sent through the Murderer's Quivering Frame.[72]" Their "eyewitness" at the execution captured the horror:

The killing of Kemmler today marks, I fear, the beginning and the end of electrocution, and it wreathes in shame the ages of the great Empire State who, entrusted with the terrific responsibility of killing a man as a man was never killed before, brought to the task imperfect machinery and turned and execution into a horror.

William Kemmler is dead, indeed, but at what a price? He has paid a double penance for his crime and a penance for his childlike trust in man who by their carelessness have brought shame upon the great State whose servants they are.

The scene of Kemmler's execution was too horrible to picture. He died the death of Feeks, the linemen, who was slowly roasted to death in the sight of thousands.

Man accustomed to every form of suffering grew faint as the awful spectacle was unfolded before their eyes. Those who stood the sight were filled with awe as they saw the effects of this most potent of fluids which is only partly understood by those who have studied it most faithfully, as it slowly, too slowly, disintegrated the fibre [sic] and tissues of the body through which it passed.

The heaving of a chest which it had been promised would be stilled in an instant peace as soon as the circuit was completed, the foaming of the mouth, the bloody sweat, the writhing shoulders and all the other signs of life.

Horrible as these were they were made infinitely more horrible by the premature removal of the electrodes and the subsequent replacing of them for not seconds but minutes, until the room was filled with the odor of burning flesh and strong men fainted and felt like logs upon the floor.

And all this done in the name of science.

It would be strange, indeed, if this execution had been anything else than what it was—a shameful thing. There has been no feature connected with the punishment of William Kemmler that was not shameful. The instruments were stolen from the first place. They were admittedly imperfect. But though the makers offered under pressure to build... machinery that could be relied upon, they were told that they were merely making a few hue and cry to save themselves.

Yesterday, with 14 months behind him in which to complete his preparations, the Warden had the execution room moved and the newly repaired voltmetre put in a place where those conducting and execution could not see it or know whether it was registering 2,000 or 200 bolts...

Nothing but a legislative inquiry will bring out the truth. And those who were present say that in the interests of humanity it is to be hoped that one will be had before another poor wretch is put on the official grill.

Kemmler went to the slaughter like a big boy, trusting and hopeful, leading ill will to none and with no apparent fear of what was coming. He chided his executioners for their nervousness and did everything in his power to help them make a good job of it.

It was not until little District Attorney Quimby, of Buffalo, came tottering down the steps, his face purpling and every fibre in his being trembling, and whispered, 'It is over,' that people knew the end had come.

In the initial attempt at execution, current was passed through Kemmler for seventeen seconds. The power was turned off and he was declared dead by Dr. Edward Charles Spitzka. But witnesses noticed that Kemmler was still breathing. Thus Spitzka and the other attending physician, Dr. Charles F. Macdonald, came forward to examine him. After confirming Kemmler was still alive, Spitzka reportedly called out, "Have the current turned on again, quick. No delay."

In the second attempt, Kemmler was shocked with 2,000 volts. Blood vessels under the skin ruptured and bled. The *New York Times* reported:

...an awful odor began to permeate the death chamber, and then, as though to cap the climax of this fearful sight, it was seen that the hair under and around the electrode on the head and the flesh under and around the electrode at the base of the spine was singeing. The stench was unbearable. [73]

Witnesses reported the smell of burning flesh and several nauseated spectators unsuccessfully tried to leave the room. In all, the entire execution took approximately eight minutes. When it was over, there was what we would call today a media storm. Competitive newspaper reporters tried to outdo one another with sensational headlines and reports. Amidst the furor, Westinghouse commented: "They would have done better using an axe."

Thus, everyone was watching the Tice execution closely. If it went badly, the electric chair as an option for capital punishment might no longer be viable.

At 6:35 A.M. on May 18, 1892, Tice was brought into the death chamber. It is not clear when he sustained the serious spinal injury that resulted in his

The Execution of Joseph Tice

Auburn Prison was constructed in 1816 on land that was originally a Cayuga Indian village. It was the site of the first execution by electric chair in 1890.

walking into the "death chamber with his cane," but it was noted repeatedly, and that he'd complained about it to his spiritual advisors the night before. In any case, he "was not able to stand erect. He gave the stick to a guard and took his seat in the chair." At 6:39 A.M., the warden gave the signal, and the current was turned on and held for fifteen seconds. The body strained inside the straps, but relaxed when the current was turned off. With half-second intervals, three additional shocks were given. There was no evidence of suffering and Tice was declared dead at 6:40 A.M.

The story of Tice's death was front-page news across the country, carried in papers like the *Pittsburg Dispatch*, the *Sedalia Weekly Bazoo* (Sedalia, Missouri), the *Washington Bee* (Washington, DC), the *Los Angeles Herald*, and the *Warren Sheaf* (Marshall County, Minnesota.) Many of the stories, like that of the *Evening Bulletin*, included details and contained a palpable sense of relief.

The witnesses saw no burning of flesh, no exhalation of air from the lungs, no struggle of the victim. The murdered met his fate calmly. The electric current was turned into the body four times, each contact being brief. The physician in charge believed that better results would be obtained in this way than with two long contacts. The complete time of contact was fifty seconds...

All the physicians examined the body and all agree that Tice had passed into eternity the instant the first contact was made. Electrician Davis said that the indicator showed 1,720 volts on the first contact with a very slightly falling off when the other three circuits were made. A closer examination of the body showed no marks or burns upon it...

Dr. Ruf declared that the electrocution was perfection itself.

Dr. George E. Fell, of Buffalo, who also witnessed the Kemmler execution, said: 'The execution of Tice can not be improved upon...There was nothing revolting in this case. As compared with the Kemmler case this was the more satisfactory. In the execution of Tice there were absolutely no reflex movements from the beginning to end, aside from the rigidity of the body produced by the breaking of the current. I was one of the first to advocate electrical execution, and, after seeing this execution, I am satisfied that he grounds I assumed were correct. There is no method comparable to it, which this case demonstrates. [74]

In fact, Fell was attending the execution in an official capacity. He was an advocate for death by electric chair, and said a month later, to a session of the American Medical Association, "So long as the death penalty is regarded by the law as a necessity, so long will electrocution be the most humane method of executing it."[75] He continued:

This statement is made only after the most careful observation, extending some years over this inquiry, and after having

The Execution of Joseph Tice

witnessed the execution of William Kemmler and Joseph L. Tice at Auburn, N. Y. The term 'humane' in this connection has a wider application than is generally considered. In the execution of the death penalty, the carrying out of the saddest mandate the law requires of its officers, the sense of duty has nerved them to their work. Even should they feel that the law may be overstepping its bounds in taking human life, it must be conceded that for the good of the greatest number its behests must be carried out. It should be remembered that the ends of legal justice are usually reached.

Another notable component of these accounts is an element of pity for Tice. As in other cases, there seemed to be some sense that a lesson might be drawn. And, as in the Kemmler case, alcohol seemed to play a key role in the commission of the crime.

'[Tice] was very brave,' said Chaplain Yates. 'He fulfilled his promise to Mr. Penney and myself that he would die like a man and a Christian. His last words to me were, 'Oh, if I didn't drink that whisky.'

'Put that in big type,' added Mr. Penney, with tears in his eyes. Then he said, "But for that very thing he was as good a man as any witness in this room.'

Also remarkable was Tice's equanimity. As the mask was put on he declared: "Look out there boys, you'll break my nose." But his nose was not broken. And as there was no sound from him and no bodily contortions, the electrocution was pronounced a success, ratifying its use in New York State, and eventually in many other states in the nation.

Chapter 12
The Mysterious Murder
of Anna Schumacher

Rochester's Holy Sepulchre Cemetery is some 300 acres, situated north of the city, not far from the Genesee River. In 1909, it was the scene of a horrific murder, that of Anna Schumacher, a seventeen-year old girl who had gone on a Saturday afternoon to decorate the graves of her father and sister.

Reports of the murder were carried on front pages nationwide: The *Salt Lake Herald*, the *Daily Mirror* (Marion, Ohio), the *Tacoma Times,* and the *New York Times.* We quote the latter nearly in full, because the article is remarkable not only for the case itself, but the detail that was carried in newspapers. And the publication of this detail would negatively affect the investigation the case.

The Mysterious Murder of Anna Schumacher

The badly bruised body of Anna Schumacher, 17 years old, of 192 Cody Street, was found this morning in a shallow grave in a secluded spot just outside Holy Sepulchre Cemetery, where she had been hastily buried by the man or men who had strangled her to death.

The bruises on the girl's arms and chest showed that she had made desperate resistance. She had gone from her home to the cemetery Saturday afternoon with her hands filled with flowers to place on the graves of her father and sister.

An autopsy...conducted by Coroner's Physician Dr. John L. Hazen of Brockport, and concluded at 8 o'clock to-night, showed that death was due to strangulation, small bones in the throat having been fractured by the fingers of the girl's assailant.

It is the theory of the police that Anna Schumacher was slain either by a tramp or by some employee of the cemetery or St. Bernard's Seminary, near-by. The seminary has a large amount of land and employs a large number of laborers.

The employees of the cemetery have been rounded up and are being examined closely. The police are also arresting all suspicious characters. It is believed that the murderer bears marks of his struggle with the victim, for particles resembling skin were found under her fingernails.

The only tangible clue the police have is the spade with which the murderer dug out the hole in which the girl's body was found. This was discovered in the pump house of the Holy Sepulchre Cemetery. It was plastered with fresh earth and spattered with blood. Later in the day it was discovered that the spade had been stolen from the pig pen of St. Bernard's Seminary estate. This strengthens the belief of the police that the crime was committed by an employee of that institution.

The movements of Anna Schumacher after she left her home on Saturday afternoon have been traced past 3 o'clock of that day. A woman friend who rode with her as far as the cemetery saw her get off the car and enter the graveyard. At 3 o'clock, an hour after she entered, she was seen at the cemetery office getting water. That she was not molested until after she had performed her errand of love was shown by the presence on the graves of her father and sister of the flowers she had carried from the house. They had been placed in little glasses containing water.

When Anna did not return to her home on Saturday night her mother and brothers became alarmed and late that night visited the cemetery, and by aid of a lantern conducted a search, but without result. The search was continued on Sunday by the relatives of the victim, and later in the day the police were notified. They in turn notified the authorities of the town of Greece, in which the cemetery is located, and early this morning a determined search was begun.

Constables Friedman and Baker struck the trail first. Marks of a struggle were found, and a trail as of a body being dragged. This led to a depression in a clump of undergrowth which the officers penetrated. Sticking out of some loose earth they spied a fragment of white cloth, and they began to dig. The first evidence of the body was the feet doubled back over the trunk. Then the body was revealed. It lay in the four-foot-long excavation, face downward, the mass of hair full of sticks and grasses, indicating that her slayer had grasped her by the feet in dragging her over the ground. Underneath her face was her hat, filled with torn fragments of her underclothing and containing her purse, which her murderer had opened and rifled of the small change the girl had with her.

Lifted out of the hole, the body gave evidence of the desperate struggle the girl had made. Her left cheek was bruised, and over her eye was a fresh cut. Her chest was black and blue, and her breast was black and discolored. Her arms to the elbows were bruised, and her torn hands showed that she had fought hard. The body was quickly identified and removed to

The Mysterious Murder of Anna Schumacher

Greece constables Otto Friedman (left) and Stalhan Baker. They had followed a rabbit through the woods and discovered Anna Schumacher's body.

the Morgue. Afterward the police closed the cemetery to the public and began a search for clues.

A man who, by his manner and actions, aroused the suspicions of the officers at work on the case, was seen at 4 o'clock this afternoon at the spot where the girl's body was found. Officers began to approach the man, whereupon he turned and fled into the dense underbrush. The woods into which the man disappeared were surrounded and a telephone call for assistance was sent to Police Headquarters.

Chief of Police Quigley, who received the call, immediately dispatched two motorcycle officers, and sent three other members of the department to the scene in an automobile. At a late hour this man had not been captured.

A number of reports were received at the Schumacher home before 1 o'clock today, and after hearing them Mrs. Mary A. Schumacher declared that she suspects a workingman in the employ of the Holy Sepulchre Cemetery of having murdered her daughter.

Mrs. Schumacher based her suspicions on a report which reached her of girls having been chased by a man employed in the cemetery. Two distinct stories of women being chased in the cemetery were told to men and women who yesterday searched throughout the old and new cemeteries for clues of the girl.

'You may say for me,' said Mrs. Schumacher, 'that I have suspicions of a workingman at the cemetery as having committed this crime.'

Two of the girls who had been to the cemetery this morning returned and said that when they were searching the cemetery yesterday a man employed there said to them:

'If you don't find her…in Section H, there's no use looking for her.'

This man was described as having a plain face, blue eyes, being of medium height, and wearing a straw hat. The girls did not know his name. It is also stated that this man said that a girl answering the description of Miss Schumacher was seen in company with a tall woman wearing a pink dress, who 'acted wild.'

The two were seen n the cemetery late Saturday, and the woman in pink was seen to leave the cemetery alone about 7 o'clock. There is no clue to her identity, and whether she knows anything of the murder remains to be seen.[76]

Shortly thereafter, there seemed to have been a big break in the case. Police made an arrest. The *New York Times* reported:

The Mysterious Murder of Anna Schumacher

Jacob Wolfsohn, 25 years old, a garment worker of 402 Carpenter Street, told in the City Hall to-night (sic), of having murdered Anna Schumacher, whose body was found near Rochester cemetery in August, 1969 [sic]. The prisoner amplified his confession by giving details of the crime, saying he strangled his victim to death, found a grave digger's spade nearby and buried the body in a wood adjourning the graveyard..

Pictured here is a Civil War Monument located in Holy Sepulchre Cemetery. Anna Schumacher was murdered just to the right of the memorial.

Detectives who listened to the narrative believed what he said and quickly sent a telegram to the Rochester police for confirmation. Pending its arrival, the prisoner was held under close surveillance by Capt. Cameron. If Wolfsohn is the right man, no time will be lost in returning him to Rochester.

Wolfsohn was arrested on a charge of looting a house at 1911 Walnut Street. He was taken to the City Hall and put in a cell there. A turnkey passing the cell noticed the man pacing up and down the floor. The attendant was afraid he was contemplating suicide, and went to the barred door.

'Bring me some paper and a pencil,' said Wolfsohn.

The request was complied with, and with trembling fingers Wolfsohn wrote the following confession: to the District Attorney—I have committed a crime in Rochester. I killed a girl in a cemetery there named Shoemaker.

A small tombstone marks the grave of Gertrude Schumacher, Anna's mother. Anna visited her grave site on the day she was murdered.

The spelling and writing were illiterate. When the writer had signed his name to the confession he seemed relived. [77]

Apparently, however, Wolfsohn's story didn't check out, as evident by another apparent break in the case. The arrest made headlines across the country,[78] when James A. Hall confessed to the crime.

The murder of Anna Schumacher in the Holy Sepulchre cemetery...has been robbed of its mystery by the confession of James Hall, the naval prisoner held on the United States prison ship Southbery on a charge of fraudulent enlistment, who says he killed the girl after assaulting her.

Hall's confession was to the effect that he was beating his way about the country last summer and on the night of Aug. 6 he was in Rochester and slept in the cemetery. He hung around next day, securing food from nearby houses and intended to sleep there that night.

Late in the afternoon he saw Anna Schumacher enter the cemetery with a bouquet of flowers for her father's grave and followed her until she was in the lonely part of the cemetery, where the grave was located. He approached the girl and made a repulsive proposal to her. She shrank from him and tried to run, but he caught her and stifled her cries while he assaulted her. This accomplished, he murdered her, although in his confession, he claims that the killing was an accident, that he only intended to stun her....

When he found she was dead he became frightened and sought for some means of disposing of the body and while searching about the vicinity of the crime he came upon a shallow grave in the sand that had been dug by some boys at play. Into this he threw the mangled body of his victim and covered it with several inches of sand. He made his way to the tracks of a railroad, where he caught a freight train and was well on his way west before the body of his victim was discovered, 48 hours after the crime.

Hall comes originally from Minnesota, is of Swedish birth and about 26 years of age. Hall is not his right name, but he was brought up by a family named Hall and

Anna Schumacher's body was found in this makeshift grave. She had been raped, mutilated, and murdered.

has always gone by that name. His real name, which he has never used, he did not give.[79]

Hall was soon turned over to Sheriff Gillette of Rochester, who traveled to Portsmouth, New Hampshire, to take custody of him. A newspaper reported that Hall was "apparently unconcerned as he left the prison ship for the train, and merely asked the sheriff how long the ride would be."[80] The reason for Hall's nonchalance was soon made clear. Hall's confession was proved false.[81] Again, papers across the country picked up the story.

> *In his plan to outdo a naval prison sentence for false enlistment, James Hall, who made a fake confession of the murder of Anna Schumacher, of Rochester, New York, is back here today, a prisoner on the United States prison ship Southbery. Hall will probably have his term lengthened as the early fruit of his trick.*[82]

And this, unfortunately, is where the story ends. As far as can be determined, there are no further mentions of Anna Schumacher — or her murderer — in the public record. Her murder remains unsolved to this day.

Chapter 13

The Unsolved Linden Murders

Today, Linden is a hamlet, a cluster of homes tucked among tree-covered hills in south-central Genesee County. It is near no major highways, nor does it have a church, school, gas station, or post office. A single railroad track bisects the community. In the 1920s, Linden was a small farming community consisting of about one hundred residents living on small family-operated farms. It had a general store, a post office, a railroad station, a mill, and a blacksmith. It was a close-knit community where everyone knew each other. They helped each other as needed and were aware of their neighbors' habits and who their friends and relatives were. Many residents gathered at the Morse General Store after evening chores to listen to the radio and discuss activities of the day. Just over ninety years ago, Linden became the center of nationwide media attention when, during a period of only five years, a series of murders were committed.

The murders struck terror into the hearts of Linden residents. Despite massive investigation efforts, the crimes were never solved. No motive was unearthed. No suspect was arrested. No trial was ever held.[83]

Unidentified Victim

Though most newspapers don't mention the first case, the Linden murders began in 1917 when an unidentified woman was found in a local farmer's woods after she had been beaten to death. At the time it was thought that an itinerant peddler had committed the crime. It was supposed that he had quickly left on a local train. The woman was never identified and her murder was never charged.

Francine (Franc) Kimball

Five years later on October 16, 1922, Francine Kimball, a frail seventy-three-year-old spinster, was killed in her home. A later student of the crime described the events in detail:

> *Charles Speed, her nearest neighbor, went to the house at about 8:00 A.M. on the seventeenth and found the house locked and no one about. He returned an hour later. Still finding no one home, he became alarmed. He told his wife, who called Mrs. Kimball's best friend, Miss Grace Smith, who along with Mrs. Robert McWithey went to the home, but a search of out buildings and the home failed to locate her. They then called Justice Maurice Nelan, who went to the location, also conducting a search to no avail. They found the telephone line had been cut and contacted the state police. Troopers arrived and scoured the entire property in vain.*
>
> *Finally, making a search of the cellar, Corporal White lit a dark area with his flashlight and saw the body stuffed under a shelf, covered with an old door. Her head had been smashed in with a heavy object. The time of her death was established to be about 6 P.M. on the sixteenth. Percy Fleming, a Linden resident, had seen her in the yard at 5:30 P.M., as he passed by the home.*
>
> *And her cow had not been milked. This was something she did faithfully at 6 P.M. daily.*

The Thomas Whaley House in Linden, New York, was the scene of a horrific triple murder. Both visible first floor windows were broken perhaps allowing the killer to gain entry to the house.

Sheriff Elliott, District Attorney, and Captain Robinson were notified and Coroner War Manchester responded to the scene. William Doyel of the Doyel Detective Agency, Rochester, NY was retained to conduct the investigation. Mrs. Kimball's two elderly brothers had been away picking apples at the time of the murder. Police could find no clues to help identify the killer. State troopers grilled everyone that lived within a mile of the crime scene.

The Batavia Daily News *offered a one-hundred-dollar reward for information leading to the arrest of the perpetrator. On October 21, Carl Meyers, a cousin of the dead woman, found a sharp, pointed rock with dried blood and gray hair on it. It was found in the cellar of the crime scene and it was determined to have been the murder weapon. It was theorized*

that whoever the killer was, he had been acquainted with the
house. After the murder, the killer locked all the windows and
doors, then left from a front door, locking it upon departing.[84]

A local newspaper disclosed one detail, apparently reported by an eyewitness, but not found in later accounts:

Late on Monday evening an automobile was driven into the
Kimball farm and stood for a short time among the trees.[85]

It is not clear whether this car was later identified and there was determined to be an innocent explanation for it, though it is important for later theories of the case. A week or so later, the County of Genesee Board of Supervisors posted a reward of one thousand dollars for information leading to an arrest. No one stepped forward to identify the killer.

Thomas Whaley, Hattie Whaley, and Mable Morse

Seventeen months later, on March 11, 1924, three more residents of Linden were brutally slain.

Thomas and Hattie Whaley lived in a home in the center of the village. That afternoon, Mable Morse, the wife of the proprietor of the general store, went to their home. When Mrs. Morse had not returned by the time a popular radio program was starting, one of her employees went looking for her. He found the Whaley house on fire. When the flames were put out, a gruesome discovery was made.

Newspapers provided considerable detail and immediately linked the case to the Kimball slaying the previous year.

Three murdered victims is the result of an act by a person who
is thought to be of a maniacal turn of mind, living in or near
the little hamlet of Linden just over the north county line of
Wyoming [C]ounty. About 7 o'clock Tuesday night the bodies
of Mr. and Mrs. Thomas A. Whaley and Mrs. George Morse
were found in the Whaley home located near the center of the

village and when discovered by Myron Smith the house had been fired with the intention of covering the crime.

The murdered persons are Thomas A. Whaley, 65 years of age and for many years has been a section boss on the Erie railroad. His wife was 58 years of age. Mrs. George Morse, age 51 is the wife of the proprietor of the general store in Linden and is well known to many friends in this county.

It was in Mr. and .Mrs. Whaley's little home, where they lived by themselves, that the triple killing took place. Mrs. Morse had gone there to get milk, as had been her custom, and evidently surprised the murder at work. Definite facts established at the autopsy were that Mrs. Morse was clubbed to death and both Mr. and Mrs. Whaley were the victims of 32-calibre bullets fired by the murderer. Mrs. Morse's body bore no marks and was not disfigured in anyway, aside from the mashing of the head with the club-like instrument. Two bullets and empty cartridge shells were found in the house.

Timely discovery of the fire by Myron Smith, a young man employed as a clerk in the Morse store, prevented the flames from gaining any great headway. The bodies of the three persons were all more or less scorched and blackened and some of the clothing was burned off them, but they were not burned beyond recognition. The flames were extinguished by neighbors with pails of water before the building got burning fast.

Mrs. Morse left her store for the Whaley house at 6:30 o'clock in the evening, taking her milk pail with her. During her absence a group of the villagers gathered in the general store to listen to a radio program, which Mrs. Morse also was to have heard. Fearing she would not return in time for the entertainment, Smith said, he went to the Whaley home to find out if she intended to come back. He was accompanied by another young man, Milton Kettle, son of Charles Kettle, who worked on the section with Mr. Whaley.

Mr. Whaley had not been feeling well for several days and Smith thought she might have decided to stay at the Whaley home on this account. When he reached the place he found the curtains drawn on all the windows and when he tried the door he found it locked. Peering into the house he saw clouds of smoke rolling about the interior. He helped young Kettle break through a window and he burst open the rear kitchen door, he told the authorities.

Horror stricken at the sight that met their eyes in the small bedroom on the first floor, the young men rushed from the house and spread the alarm. Pandemonium broke loose among the assemblage waiting at the store and within a short time the men of the village put out the fire with palls of water and telephoned the state troopers in Batavia.

Upon the arrival of the authorities and their investigation of the crime, it was at once evident that the three persons had been killed or nearly killed in other rooms and dragged to the bedroom, where they were finished off with the new handle of a pickax. Around the bodies was wrapped paper and bed clothing, all saturated in kerosene oil, which was probably obtained from a can found in the house. So well had the murderer prepared to fire the house that the clothing was still smoldering when the authorities arrived.

From bullet marks, blood splotches and other results of the murderer's work, a story of .what probably happened has been reconstructed.

The murderer locked all the doors to prevent any interruption while at his gruesome task of disposing of the three bodies. He pulled down all the window shades. On the window of the front kitchen door, where there were [sic] no shade, but a neat muslin curtain, he nailed a piece of cloth.

The Whaley house bedroom where the murders took place. An axe handle used to kill Mrs. Morse is propped between the door frames.

Circumstances surrounding the Whaley–Morse murder are identical in many important particulars with those of the murder of Frances L. Kimball on the afternoon of Monday, October 16, 1922 and the strange effort to burn the home of Justice of the Peace Maurice Nelan, adjoining the Kimball place on Sunday morning September 23, 1923.

Melvin Whaley of this village who lives in the Prentice house on South Main street adjoining the Prentice farm is a brother of Thomas Whaley the murdered man. Mr. Morse has offered a reward of a $1,000 for the capture of the murderer of his wife, and it is expected that the county of Genesee will double the amount, Up to the time of going to press no arrests have been made.[86]

An autopsy would show that Thomas Whaley, a section hand on the Erie Railroad that ran behind his home, had been shot in the neck. His wife had sustained a single gunshot wound in her head. Mrs. Morse had been clubbed to death with an axe handle.

Authorities theorized that the murderer might have been using the railroad to get in and out of town, as no car had been spotted, as in the Kimball murder.

One student of the crime put it this way:

An intense investigation followed. Several tramps, a common sight along the railroad in Linden, were questioned. Linden was overrun by police (the Genesee County Sheriff's Department and the fairly-new New York State Police shared the investigation), reporters from throughout Western New York, and even sightseers who clogged the narrow snow-rutted roads.

As word spread in the hamlet, women gathered to comfort each other and farmers bolted their doors and armed themselves out of fear....

Troopers were called immediately and...Buffalo Police Captain Joseph Whitwell, chief of the Bertillon Bureau and a noted fingerprint expert, was retained and went to the scene.

Fingerprints taken at the scene were of no value because they had been damaged by water from putting out the fire. Some felt the murders were the result of a robbery, as the purses had been emptied and watches were missing. Others thought it was a maniac who had traveled along the railroad line. As the investigation proceeded, police became more convinced that he murdered was a local resident and concentrated their efforts on that theory.

No one was allowed to leave the area unless first checked by police. As word spread, thrill-seekers from Batavia, Buffalo, and Rochester poured into the area, impeding the investigation by causing traffic jams. Local people were interviewed and re-interviewed with no solid leads developed. The captain had

*a trooper presence in Linden at all times with one trooper
assigned to the hamlet, available for immediate duty, and two
others on horse patrol around the perimeter. It was suggested
by an investigator that a picture of the murdered victim's eyes
be taken with the belief that an image of the killer would be
imprinted on the eyeball as the last vision of the victim. It
was no joke and was reported in a national weekly review to
have been used in several important criminal investigations.
Again, as in the Kimball murder, time passed with the crimes
never being solved.[87]*

As fear and interest in the case were so high, the available rewards
grew. Rochester's *Democrat and Chronicle* noted:

*Radio was invoked tonight by the authorities investigating
the brutal murder of Mr. and Mrs. Thomas Whaley and*

Photo of John Vetosky, recently released from Dannemora State Hospital for the Criminally
Insane. He would confess to the Linden slayings but later recanted and was cleared.

their neighbor, Mrs. George W. Morse...Offers of rewards aggregating more than $8,000 were broadcast to thousands of listeners all over the country from station...operated by the Democrat and Chronicle *and the* Times-Union *of Rochester.*

Meeting in executive session late this afternoon the Genesee Board of Supervisors passed unanimously a resolution offering...the town of Bethany, in which Linden is located, $5,000 cash to the person furnishing information leading to the arrest and conviction of the slayers.

Already an offer of $1,000 had been made by George W. Morse...of this village, husband of one of the victims. In addition...the Board of Supervisors, announcement of the offer of $1,000 for the arrest of the murderer of Miss Frances Kimball, aged spinster, in Linden two years ago, still stood.[88]

In March 1924, John Vetosky, who was recently released from the Dannemora State Hospital for the Criminal Insane, confessed to the Linden slayings.[89] He apparently gave a reasonable account of how he committed the crimes, but he later recanted[90] and his alibi was confirmed. Though his name continued to surface occasionally in connection with the case, it does not appear that authorities believed he was the guilty party.[91]

The community remained anxious. In the summer of 1924, a local newspaper printed a story under the headline "Death Letter Causes Fear: Anonymous Letters Received Since Death of Whaley Disturb Residents of Linden."

Surrounded at all times with the mystery of four brutal murders, anonymous letters are now being received with forebodings of others to follow. Postmaster Ira J. Page Saturday received one from 'A Friend' and postmarked Detroit, Mich.

This letter asks him to warn the village of an impending fifth murder. The letter says that a fifth is being planned. The communication urges the postmaster to notify the authorities to be on their guard and to 'watch and pray.' Several anonymous letters have so far been received since the slaying of Mr. and Mrs. Thomas A. Whaley and Mrs. George W. Morris on March 11, and the brutal killing of Miss Frances Kimball.[92]

Gradually, the frenzy abated. The newspaper headlines grew smaller. Soon enough, the *Daily News* edition of March 11, 1925, was marking the one-year after the triple slaying. They summarized events and noted that "Genesee County authorities and clever detectives carried on during the next several weeks (after the murders) the most thorough murder investigations that could possibly be made, but the Linden slayer still goes unapprehended." [Sic]

It was eventually thought that a tramp, perhaps travelling through Linden by rail, had committed the crimes. The murders remain unsolved to this day.

No clear connections, if there were any, were ever deduced between the murder of the unknown woman in 1917, the Kimball murder of 1922, and the triple slayings of 1924. Over time, they became known as the "Unsolved Linden Murders." No one was ever arrested for any of these five murders. No motive was ever found, nor was the identity of the murderer or murderers ever determined. Gruesome and perplexing as they were, the Linden murders soon faded from the public's memory.

Notes

1 William Farley Peck, *History of Rochester and Monroe County, New York: From the Earliest Times to the Beginning of 1907* (New York: Pioneer Publishing, 1908), p. 23–24.

2 Ibid.

3 See http://darkdestinations.blogspot.com/2009/09/torture-tree.html. For photos of graves and monuments, see Steve Collward's piece at http://www.captainselinscompany.org/grovlnd.html. Also see George S. Conover, ed., *Journals of the Military Expedition of Major General John Sullivan against the Six Nations of Indians in 1779 with Records of Centennial Celebrations* (Auburn, N.Y.: Knapp, Peck & Thompson Printers, 1887); Joseph R. Fischer, *A Well Executed Failure: The Sullivan Campaign Against the Iroquois, July–September 1779* (Columbia, SC: Univ. of South Carolina Press, 1997); Otis G. Hammond, ed., *Letters and Papers of Major-General John Sullivan, Continental Army* (Concord, NH: New Hampshire Historical Society, 1939); *The Sullivan-Clinton Campaign in 1779, Chronology and Selected Documents* (Albany: Univ. of the State of New York, 1929); Glenn E. Williams, *Year of the Hangman, George Washington's Campaign Against the Iroquois* (Yardley, PA: Westholme Publishing, 2005.)

4 Lockwood Lyon Doty, *A History of Livingston County, New York, from its Earliest Traditions to its Part in the War for our Union: with an Account of*

the Seneca Nation of Indians, and Biographical Sketches of Earliest Settlers and Prominent Public Men (Geneseo, New York: Edward E. Doty, 1876), 508.

5   Roger Larson, a relative of Archibald MacLachlan, has done considerable research on this case. See http://www.correctionhistory.org/html/chronicl/hangedtwice/jamesmclean.html. Accessed November 15, 2011.

6   Details taken from an account on the Genesee County website, accessed June 2011. The page no longer appears to be active. http://www.co.genesee.ny.us/dpt/historian/hangings.html.

7   Ibid.

8   Larson, Ibid. For a useful discussion of the term "gibbet" (which Larson uses in a non-standard form), see http://www.executedtoday.com/2008/08/28/1807-james-mclean-twice/. Accessed November 15, 2011.

9   Larson, Ibid.

10   Testimony taken from original court transcript and "Outrage Unparalleled in Rochester—Assassination!" in *The Daily Advertiser*, October 30, 1837.

11   "The Expositor Office," at http://www.lds-mormon.com/06.shtml. Accessed January 25, 2012.

12   Greg West, "Liberal or Conservative? Joseph Smith's 1844 Presidential Platform," at http://www.ldsliberty.org/liberal-or-conservative-joseph-smiths-1844-presidential-platform/. Accessed January 26, 2012:

13   Arnold K. Garr, "Joseph Smith: Campaign for President of the United States," at http://lds.org/ensign/2009/02/joseph-smith-campaign-for-president-of-the-united-states?lang=eng. Accessed January 27, 2012.

14   "The Expositor Office," Ibid.

15   Paul Malczewki, "The Heinous High Falls Murder," in *Epitaph* (Rochester, New York), Spring 1999, at http://www.lib.rochester.edu/index.cfm?PAGE=3102. Accessed June 22, 2011.

Notes

16 Ibid.

17 Ibid.

18 Ibid.

19 Peck, Ibid.

20 Malczewki, Ibid.

21 Quoted in Malczewki, Ibid.

22 Malczewki, Ibid.

23 Malczewki, Ibid.

24 "Extraordinary Letter from a Murderer," *Nashville Union and American*, May 20, 1858, p. 1.

25 Ibid.

26 Peck, Ibid., p. 172.

27 "Another Murder Trial at Rochester—The Case of Manley Locke," The *New York Times*, October 12, 1858.

28 Ibid.

29 Ibid.

30 "The Locke Trial," *Genesee County Herald*, October 30, 1858, p. 1.

31 "Escape of Fifteen Prisoners from Jail—Manley Locke at Large Again," The *Geneva Gazette*, December 17, 1858, p. 1. See also "Fifteen Prisoners Escape," *Cataraugus Republican* (Ellicotville, New York)(no month or day on page; 1858.)

32 "Sentence of Manley Locke to the Auburn State Prison for Life," *Genesee County Herald*, January 6, 1859, p. 1.

33 Cindy Amrhein and Ellen Bachorski, *Bread and Butter: The Murders*

of Polly Frisch. (See http://www.rootsweb.ancestry.com/~nycalaba/Polly.html.) Select chapters available at http://www.correctionhistory.org/html/chronicl/polly/. Both accessed December 13, 2011.

34 The *Genesee Democrat,* November 14, 1857, p. 1.

35 "Trial of Polly Frisch: For the Murder of Her Former Husband, Henry Hoag, by the Administration of Arsenic," in K.W. Beers, *Gazetteer and Biographical Record of Genesee County, N.Y., 1788–1890* (Syracuse, N.Y.: J.W. Vose & Co., 1890.)

36 Martin H. Bovee, *Reasons for Abolishing Capital Punishment* (Chicago: A.J. Cox and Co., 1878), p. 122–123.

37 Ibid. p. 121–123, passim.

38 "Commutation of the Sentence of Polly Frisch," the *Daily Herald* (Batavia, New York), 1859 (month and day obscured.)

39 *Documents of the State of New York*, Vol. 6 (Albany, N.Y.: C. Van Benthuyson, 1860): 130.

40 "Polly Frisch Pardoned: She Had Been in Prison for More than Thirty-Three Years," the *New York Times*, December 10, 1892.

41 *The Illustrated American,* Vol. 13: 20.

42 *Charles Eighmey: His Life and Trial, And Account of Execution, From the Official Notes of F.H. Harris, Court Stenographer* (Canandaigua, New York: C. Jobson, Printer, 1876.), p. 1.

43 "Probable Fatal Affray in Phelps!" the *Geneva Gazette,* July 3, 1874.

44 "Murder," the *Geneva Courier*, July 8, 1874, p. 1.

45 Ibid.

46 *Charles Eighmey*, Ibid., p. 2.

47 Ibid.

Notes

48 "The Murder Trial: Testimony in the Case of Chas. Eighmey," the *Geneva Courier* May 19, 1875, p. 1.

49 Kevin A. Cotter, *The Lurking Devil of Murder.* See http://www. charleseighmey.com.

50 *Charles Eighmey*, Ibid., p. 2–3.

51 Ibid., p. 6–7.

52 Ibid., p. 14–16, passim.

53 Ibid., p. 18, passim..

54 Ibid., p. 22, passim.

55 The *Utica Morning Herald*, September 2, 1876.

56 Ibid., p. 3.

57 "The Gallows: Execution of Charles Eighmey," the *Geneva Courier*, September 13, 1876, p. 1.

58 Ibid.

59 "The Gallows: A Murderer's Last Words to His Accusers," the *National Republican* (Washington, DC), September 9, 1876, p. 1.

60 "The Gallows: Execution of Charles Eighmey," Ibid.

61 Ibid.

62 *French's Gazetteer of New York State*, 1860. See http://www.rootsweb. ancestry.com/~nyliving/town/avon.htm. Accessed December 13, 2011.

63 "A Delayed Hanging: The Crime for Which William Pierson has Vainly Tried to Escape Death," the *New York Times,* July 1, 1879.

64 "The Doomed Man," *Mt. Morris Enterprise*, March 20, 1880.

65 "Crime and Its Penalties: The Hanging of William Pierson," the *New*

Notes

York Times, March 20, 1880.

66 Austin Abbott, *Select Cases on the Law of Evidence as Applied during the Examination of Witness* (The Diossy Law Book Co., 1895), p. 122–123.

67 "The Doomed Man!: How He Passed His Last Night" *Mt. Morris Enterprise*, March 20, 1880, p. 1

68 Ibid.

69 "Death Sentence," *Mt. Morris Enterprise*, March 9, 1878.

70 "Tragedy in a Railroad Station: A German Woman Kills Her Child and Seriously Wounds Herself," The *New York Times,* January 2, 1885.

71 "Rochester History, an Illustrated Timeline." See http://www.vintageviews.org/vv-tl/index.htm. Accessed February 22, 2012.

72 "The First Execution by Electrocution in Electric Chair: Kemmler's Death by Torture; Twice the Current Was Sent through the Murderers Quivering Frame," the *New York Herald*, August 7, 1890. The series of subheads told the story: Breathed After First Shock; Doctors Pronounced Him Dead and Then to Their Horror Discovered Their Mistake; Witnesses Faint and Sick: Terror Added to the Scene by the Burning Parts of the Body; Disagreement of Scientists: Not Satisfied That the New Method of Execution is a Success. Full text available at http://www.mindfully.org/Reform/Kemmler-Torture-Death7aug1890.htm. Accessed December 13, 2011.

73 "Far Worse than Hanging," the *New York Times*, August 7, 1890, p. 1.

74 "Legal Execution: Another Murderer Pays the Death Penalty in New York; Electricity Did the Work," *The Evening Bulletin* (Maysville, Kentucky), May 19, 1892, p. 1.

75 George F. Fell, "Electrodes, and their Application in Electrocution," Read in the Section of Neurology and Medical Jurisprudence, at the Forty-third Annual Meeting of the American Medical Association, held at Detroit, Mich., June, 1892. Available at http://jama.ama-assn.org/content/XIX/13/365. extract. Accessed December 13, 2011.

Notes

76 "Girl Slain After Decorating Graves: Anna Schumacher, 17 Years Old, Strangled in Rochester Cemetery and Crudely Buried," the *New York Times*, August 10, 1909, p.1. .

77 "Confesses Girl's Murder: Wolfsohn Says He Killed Anna Schumacher near Rochester," the *New York Times*, September 20, 1909, p. 1.

78 "Rochester Cemetery Mystery Laid Bare: Work of Swedish Tramp," the *Marion Daily Mirror* (Marion, Ohio), January 24, 1910, p. 1.

79 "Naval Recruit Admits Murder: James Hall Clears Mystery of Rochester Cemetery," the *Democratic Banner* (Mt. Vernon, Ohio) January 25, 1910, p. 1.

80 "Turned Over to Sheriff: James A. Hall, Confessed Murderer of Miss Anna Schumacher, Surrendered by Federal Officers," the *Palestine Daily Herald* (Palestine, Texas) January 24, 1910, p. 1.

81 "To Court Martial Hall for Murder Confession," the *Los Angeles Herald*, March 5, 1910, p. 1.

82 "Hall Back on Prison Ship," the *Marion Daily Mirror*, February 11, 1910 p. 1.

83 William F. Brown, "The Linden Murders" [publication data not given.] See http://off-beat-history.wny.org/local.htm. Accessed January 12, 2012.

84 Albert S. Kurek, *The Troopers are Coming: New York State Troopers, 1917*–1943 (Bloomington, IN: Rooftop Publishing, 2007), p. 148.

85 "Aged Spinster Slain in Cellar: Bleating Cow Calls Attention to Crime," the *Evening World* (New York, N.Y.), October 18, 1922, p. 3.

86 Supposed Maniac Kills Three Persons on Tuesday Night at Linden: Attempt to Conceal Heinous Crime, Setting Fire to Bodies in House," the *Wyoming County Times* (Warsaw, N.Y.), March 13, 1924, p. 1.

87 Kurek, Ibid.

Notes

88 "Radio Broadcasts Reward Totalling $8,000 in Search for Linden Murderer," *Democrat and Chronicle* (Rochester, N.Y.), March 14, 1924, p. 1.

89 "Confesses to Linden Murders: John Vetoski Arrested at Perry, Tells Blood Curdling Story," the *Dansville Breeze* (Dansville, New York), March 18, 1924, p. 1.

90 Linden Murder Still Unsolved; Alibi Offered by 'Confessed Slayer' Substantiated by Reliable Farmers," the *Morning Herald* (Gloversville, N.Y.), March 20, 1924, p. 1.

91 "Train Rider Confesses Looting Mail Sacks in Rail Station at Warsaw: Vetosky Tells Police He Got Clothing from Parcel—Once Confessed to Linden Murders—Admits Breaking from Pen," the *Morning Express* (Buffalo, New York), May 18, 1926, p. 1.

92 "Death Letter Causes Fear: Anonymous Letters Received since Death of Whaley Disturb Residents of Linden," the *Evening Leader* (Corning, New York), August 25, 1924 (page number obscured in online database.)

About the Author

Michael Keene worked for twenty-five years in the financial services industry as a financial advisor. He is the author of *Folklore and Legends of Rochester, The Mystery of Hoodoo Corner* and *Mad~House*. He is also the producer of the award-winning documentary series, *Visions- True Stories of Spiritualism, Secret Societies & Murder*. He lives in Pittsford, New York with his wife Diana, their daughter Michele, and their grandson, Joshua. His website address is http://www.ad-hoc-productions.com and email is: info@ad-hoc-visions.com

Also by Michael Keene

VISIONS

TRUE STORIES OF SPIRITUALISM, SECRET SOCIETIES AND MURDER

Through the use of beautifully crafted illustrations, award-winning animation, live action sequences, and a thrilling musical score, we are taken on a journey through time while unraveling three more true stories of crime and punishment in Western New York.

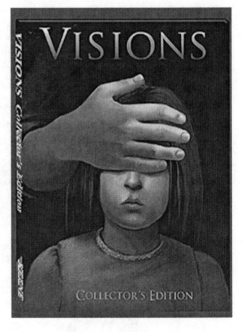

CPSIA information can be obtained
at www.ICGtesting.com
Printed in the USA
FFOW01n1637210116
20593FF